nothing
something to believe in

nica lalli

Prometheus Books

59 John Glenn Drive
Amherst, New York 14228-2197

Published 2007 by Prometheus Books

Inquiries should be addressed to
Prometheus Books
59 John Glenn Drive
Amherst, New York 14228–2197
VOICE: 716–691–0133, ext. 207
FAX: 716–564–2711
WWW.PROMETHEUSBOOKS.COM

11 10 09 08 07   5 4 3 2 1

Library of Congress Cataloging-in-Publication Data

Lalli, Nica.
    Nothing: something to believe in / by Nica Lalli.
        p. cm.
    ISBN: 978–1–59102–529–0 (alk. paper)
    1. Lalli, Nica. 2. Atheists—United States—Biography. I. Title.

BL2790.L35A3 2007
211'.8092—dc22
[B]   2006102724

Printed in the United States on acid-free paper

Events in this book have been filtered through the lens of the author's experience and are based on the author's memory of them. Some names, places, and details have been altered.

For Greg, Amelia, and Victor

"... *because instead of nothing there is what there is.*"

—William Trevor, *The Story of Lucy Gault*

contents

8   contents

acknowledgments

I never thought I would write a book. When I came up with the idea, I was frightened by the thought that I might try and fail, or, worse, that I might never try at all. I have my husband, Greg, to thank for urging me to start, and for reading, editing, and continuing to encourage me all the way through. I want to thank my kids, Amelia and Victor, who put up with me sitting at my desk for too many hours, who forgave me for hogging the family computer, and who have been my cheerleaders from the beginning. My sister, Gina, has given me much-needed insight about growing up, as only a sister can do, and as an early reader she helped me refine many portions of the book.

I have many friends who knew me as a painter, a teacher, or a mom, and who quickly rallied around the idea of me being a writer. In particular, Deborah Jaffe (my oldest friend) and Vicki Belun (one of my newest) read the early versions and gave me advice and support. And I must also thank all the other readers: Linda Aponte, Catherine Teegarden, Sarah Butterworth, Bill Bonnell, Cindy Hanson, and Cynthia Sweeney. Their responses to my drafts were always positive, constructive, and kept me on track. I would also like to thank Roberta Rubien; the work I did with her was invaluable to many parts of my life.

I was lucky to have people who did more than encourage. I had friends who challenged me, pushed me, and advised me about the ways of the publishing world. Those people are: Stuart Miller, who kept me at it when I almost gave up; David Drake, who gave me the help many others would not; Lev Fruchter, who acted like the agent he used to be; and Christopher Schelling, who told me to keep trying and gave me hope. I also want to thank Prometheus Books for publishing this memoir. Everyone there has been helpful and I have enjoyed working with the staff.

Lastly, I want to thank my family. My sister, my parents, and my extended family have all been eager to read my story and be a part of my journey. I especially want to thank my parents, Lex Lalli and Lou Lalli, for all they have done and continue to do for me.

I also want to thank my husband's family. My mother-in-law has always been a supporter, and her willingness to accept me and take me into her family so readily has always been a source of strength. My sister-in-law and her husband are part of the reason I wrote this book, and for that I am grateful. Had they not pushed me to define my beliefs, I might never have thought it through carefully enough to write about it, nor would I have been as confident as I have become in being nothing.

introduction

muslims? They've got it easy. Gays? Relatively speaking, life's a party. You know who the true outsiders are in American society?

Nonbelievers.

A recent study by University of Minnesota sociology professors on the tolerance of "others" in America showed that the group most hated and feared, the group seen as the greatest threat to our country, is atheists. The study also said that nonbelievers are the one group that Americans would least like to have marry into their family.

I have been living with this kind of reaction to my beliefs—in nothing—my whole life. And after watching our country grow ever more fundamentalist on issues like a woman's right to choose and in stories like the Terri Schiavo saga; after seeing this nation led into war by a president who believed God put him in charge for just such a crusade, I finally felt the need to tell my story, my evolution of becoming a nothing.

I like the word *nothing* because it makes no reference to a god; it cuts out that root (*theo*) to stand on its own. I decided to share my journey and show people that I could be sure of my beliefs and my convictions, even if they are not based on a holy book, a messiah, or any organized church. But before I could write anything, I had to find out how I had gotten to the point of needing to have an identity. So, after spending many years defining myself as what I was not, I decided to find out what I was, what I am.

I sat down one sunny May afternoon and made a list of all the times in my life I had come into contact with religion. I had to go back pretty far and I realized that for most of my life, I was frightened or upset by religion. Growing up, I had no religious identity and so I had no point of understanding when I did come face to face with religion or religious people. I had no ammunition against people who wanted me to join them, who needed me to see things through the lens of their religions. As I grew older, I was ready to defend my right to be whomever and whatever I wanted to be, but I lacked the vocabulary to define my position. I was at a loss when challenged, and so I got frustrated and angry at the people who kept at me, those who wanted me to become what they were. This was complicated because those people were my in-laws.

Being hated by the vague idea of "the majority of Americans" is one thing; being despised by your own family is another. In fairness, my sister-in-law and her husband claim that they do not hate me, nor did they mean to disrespect me when they challenged my beliefs and told me I was wrong to have any belief other than the one they had, the belief in Jesus Christ as savior. However, they did not find a way to accept me or to understand me, and they made it clear that unless I converted to Christianity, there could be no real friendship and maybe not even familial cordiality. Years went by with almost no contact, and no attempts were made to address our differences. In the past few years we have had some get-togethers, but there is still much unsaid and many issues unresolved.

I wrote this book as a way to respond to my in-laws and people like them. I needed to find my voice. I needed to find comfort in the word *nothing*; I wanted to own it instead of hide from it. As I looked at the list I made, I started to see chapters of a book, and the chapters started to add up to a better understanding of who I was, how I had gotten here, and what it was that I did believe in.

As I wrote, the religious issues in America swirled around me. With the success of the movie *The Passion of the Christ*, the insistent post 9/11 tradition of singing "God Bless America" at the seventh-inning stretch of every Yankee game, and the debates over the ethics of stem cell research, America has become more polarized over issues of belief. Suddenly what had been a family feud gained resonance on a larger scale. And in the end, the real question, to my in-laws and to the rest of my country, is: can't we all just agree to disagree and learn to get along?

I do not pretend to be the voice for all the "others"; I can only speak for myself. And yet I do hope that my story can add to a productive dialogue and illuminate what some find to be offensive. In the end, tolerance is our best shot toward either family togetherness or national and global tranquility. And without understanding, tolerance cannot exist. Somehow it seems that many of those who follow the words of such wise men as Jesus or Muhammad skip the parts where these issues are raised. Somehow the fundamentalists miss the big messages behind the religions they profess to believe in with every cell of their beings. Wars are waged, lives are lost, and I sit here being hated for my ideas. Just because I call myself nothing doesn't mean I don't have ideas. I have belief, I just don't have religion.

part 1

chapter 1

god punished me

i t's a sunny day in first grade. The sunshine falls through the enormous windows onto the desks and the floor, casting a grid across the room. My desk is near the wall opposite the window. There is a chalkboard next to me. I lean my head against it and feel the coolness of the slate. I think, "Cathy went home sick yesterday. She raised her hand and told Mrs. Clark she had a stomachache and she was sent home. Just like that. Her mom came and got her and she was home. It was so easy."

My classroom is a nice, cozy place. There is a reading area and a play area and we have desks in little rows and there are letter flash cards all around the top of the chalkboards. Each card shows the sound a letter makes or a picture of a thing that makes the sound the letter makes. "C" is a nutcracker cracking a walnut: *ck, ck.* "W" is a child blowing a dandelion puff: *whoosh, whoosh.* "S" is a flat tire: *ssss, ssss.* I love my teacher Mrs. Clark. She is pretty and nice and never yells. She tells us stories and brings us treats or special things to look at. But what I really want, on this particular day, is to see if I can get home as easily as Cathy did yesterday.

Maybe I am tired. Maybe there is a spelling test. Maybe I am going to have to read aloud because it is my turn and I don't want to stumble over the words in front of the whole class. I think about getting caught lying to Mrs. Clark. Would I get in trouble? Would she not like me anymore? But if I say it is a tummy ache, I know there's no way she could tell what is going on in my stomach, so she will never know I am lying. I decide to raise my hand and open my mouth to say, "I feel sick."

Before I know it, I am being escorted by Mary Beth to the office. Mary Beth is another student in first grade. I can't look at her because I fear she will know I am lying. So I look at the floor and hold my tummy. The principal calls my mother, and she comes to get me. "This is too easy," I think to myself as I slide in the backseat of the old green car. My little sister, Gina, is at daycare for the afternoon, so it will just be me and Mom for a few hours. I must be dreaming; this is too good to be true.

We get home and I get sympathy. I get to sit in the rocking chair in the kitchen with pillows all around me and blankets on top of me. Mom makes me tea with lots of sugar, which I drink one teaspoon at a time. Dad hates it when we drink with a spoon, but we love it. Even milk tastes better if you use a teaspoon to drink it, and it is best if you slurp the liquid off the spoon, and then sigh after you lick the spoon and put it back in the cup. So there I am, pampered, happy, and alone with my mom and the new dog.

We got a dog over the summer. He is a Standard Poodle and he is apricot-colored. He is really a kind of sandy color, but we call it apricot. He is still a puppy and he chews things and we have to keep him in the kitchen. His name is Laffy.

His real name is Lafcadio, and I don't know where my parents got that crazy name, but I do love that puppy. Dad built a door to keep him in the kitchen. It is actually a half door, a Dutch door. He said it is the kind of door they have in Holland, and I know Holland is where they have wooden shoes and windmills. I have a book about a little girl from Holland named Katrina. I love that girl and those wooden shoes. So I love the Dutch door.

The dog is at my feet and the tea is warm on my lap. Mom is busy elsewhere in the house and I am happy. The fact that I lied my way into this bliss is only a little nagging tug at one side of me. I shake my head to scatter the tug away. Anyway, I have to go to the bathroom. So I throw the blankets off and put my tea down. I have to be careful with the door so the dog does not get out. He chewed one of Mom's best shoes the other day and is still in exile. When I try to come back into the kitchen, Laffy is right there on the other side of the door. So I slam it as I reenter, to make sure he doesn't get out. I slam it hard and I yelp with pain. My finger is caught in the door. I pull my hand away and tears leap into my eyes.

"Are you okay?!" Mom yells from downstairs. "What was that noise? Stay in the chair."

I manage to answer, "I'm fine. I had to pee."

I sit back in the rocking chair, holding my finger, shaking from the pain. I cover myself back up with one hand, unable to use the hand with the smashed finger. I settle back into the chair and catch my breath. It really hurts. I look at the finger. Right under the nail is a big purple mark. It is about the size and shape of the fingernail, but it is dark-colored and puffy.

I am frozen with fear. This is my punishment for lying. I stare at the finger and start to panic. If anyone sees this, it will be a sure sign that I have lied. Everyone will know that I am bad, that I lied and God punished me.

At that moment, the fact that it was God punishing me rushed into my head without much logic. My parents never said, "God will get you for that" or "God is watching" or anything at all about God. They may have said, "Santa is watching, Santa wants you to be good," but never God. Maybe some of my friends had informed me that there was an omnipresent power ruling the earth. Maybe my friends had warned me to be good . . . or else. And there I was sitting in the kitchen with real proof that I had not been good, with a real wound as retribution.

I get up again from the chair and go to the drawer with the knives. If I can pop this blister, I can get rid of the evidence and no one would know anything had happened. I stand at the counter with a big knife in my hand. I put my hurt hand on the counter, fingers spread out so I can pop the blood blister. As I raise the knife to strike at the finger, I hear my mother on the stairs. I put the knife in the drawer and jump back in the rocking chair. As soon as she enters the room, she knows something is up. It is the incredible sixth sense of a mother to always know that there is a problem in the room.

I try to hide my hand; I do not want to reveal the mark of God to my mother. But eventually she wears me down and I tell all. I show her the blister and I tearfully tell her about Cathy going home sick and how easy it had been to get sent home and how I was sorry and how I would never lie again. She must have been angry, and yet I don't recall getting punished or yelled at. Maybe she sensed that my fear of God was enough. Even though she did not encourage my belief of the great deity, she might not have totally dispelled the notion either.

We folded the blankets and put the pillows away; there was no more rocking chair for me that day. We went to pick up my sister and nothing more was said of the day's events. The blood blister did go away . . . slowly. And after that I was terrified of being sent home sick. The next year I had a high fever and could barely keep my head off my desk. But I would not be sent home. I waited until lunchtime, and when I walked in the door, I was put to bed and stayed there for a week, feverish and delirious. No blood blisters that time, but the fear of the possibility of God was firmly planted.

nothing

I believe that I asked my parents the big religion question because I wanted to have a first Communion. I secretly hoped that they would, upon my reminding them, suddenly remember that I needed a big white dress, white gloves, shoes, and a veil. Especially the veil; I wanted that the most. I often put towels on my head to pretend I had long hair, and the veil would be an even better hair extender for my in-front-of-the-mirror fantasies. For Communion, everything was going to be white. Like the wedding dresses—big, billowy white dresses—that my friends had in their dress-up bins, dresses that had belonged to their moms. I had seen my mother's wedding picture, and, even though the picture was black and white I could tell that the dress she had worn was brown: two-tone brown and not a puff on it. It looked like something Laura Petrie would have worn to dust on the *Dick Van Dyke Show*, not at all a proper wedding dress.

I wanted that white outfit. Michelle had gotten hers. We were allowed to play with the gloves and the veil, but we couldn't even touch the dress. It had to be perfect for the first Communion: clean, pure, fresh. Michelle was going to carry a little bunch of flowers, too—white, of course—as she marched down the aisle in the church. It was going to be better than playing wedding with our favorite boyfriend, Ted, we decided. It was going to be so much more real. In a church and everything.

I knew that Michelle had to go to special classes to be able to get the dress and the bouquet and the whole thing, but I figured it wouldn't be a problem for me to catch up. If I started right away, I could learn whatever needed to be learned in a few weeks. I knew some of the stuff already, courtesy of Michelle. I knew the Lord's Prayer and the Hail Mary. I had even been allowed to hold her rosary. That was pretty, too. I would get one like hers, with pink beads and the tiny cross hanging off the end.

This won't be a problem, I reasoned, because my father is Catholic. I mean, he is Italian, and Michelle's mom said that all Italian people are Catholic, and she should know because she is from Switzerland, which I know is right next to Italy. So that will make this whole plan a cinch. Dad will realize that he forgot this whole thing and that he needs to sign me up for those classes, and before you know it, I'll be on my way. Then Mom can have a party for me, too. Michelle said that some people bring presents and even money.

I came home from my afternoon at Michelle's house ready to find out the most important thing: "What are we?" Knowing, as I did, that my father was Catholic was complicated by the fact that I also knew that my mother was Jewish. I knew that Jewish was not the same as Catholic, that it was somehow opposite. I knew that Jews were often hated and that there had been some kind of tragedy; my mother talked of huge numbers of Jews being killed a long time ago. My information was sketchy (we had not yet studied the Holocaust in second grade), but I was pretty sure that we weren't really Jewish. We couldn't be, because we celebrated Christmas, which my Jewish friend Suzy did not. Santa came and there were presents and parties. And Easter was always a big event too. The Easter Bunny came, and again there were presents and parties, along with the annual watching of *The Ten Commandments* on TV. Those strange people in robes, Moses and all those bearded guys, were Jewish, but we weren't at all like that. Yet whenever anyone asked us, "What are you? Where are you from?" we always answered, "Italian and Jewish." So I figured that Jewish was more like a nationality than a religion.

I was sure that we were not any of the other religions, either. We were certainly not Presbyterian, Lutheran, or Episcopalian. And I knew that we were not anything weird, like Hare Krishna or any other kind of robed and turbaned thing. Most of my middle-class white friends were middle-class white religions.

Now Suzy was a "real" Jew. She went to Hebrew school and celebrated Chanukah, and we even went to a Chanukah party at her house one year and had a great time. There were presents, and they had a tree just like ours, only it had little blue decorations in the shape of stars made out of two triangles, and the tinsel was all blue and white—no red or green anywhere. I found out later that this was not a Christmas tree as I had thought . . . it was a Chanukah bush. And I was very jealous of Suzy at Chanukah, because she got gifts each night for over a week, plus she got Christmas presents. But I would deal with that after I had cleared up the big question about our family. First I had to find out what we were and then I could work on adding any other traditions that would increase my gift load.

I was far less interested in my other friends' spiritual lives. Being a Presbyterian did not seem to have much appeal. No white dresses, no extra gifts. And the same went for all those other churches. I was not crazy about those churches anyway; I thought they were odd places. I had been in them for Brownies. We met in a church basement, and it seemed dark and creepy. And summer camp was in a church. That was nice enough, but we never went into the church part of the church; we were always on the side, in the recreation hall or in the gymnasium; it wasn't churchlike at all. Plus I knew that there was not much chance that my parents would say we were any of *those* religions. Not when I was quite sure that we almost certainly had to be Catholic.

I decided to wait until after dinner to ask the big question. Somehow I sensed that it *was* a big question: "What are we?" It sounded pretty big, and I figured it deserved a good answer.

My sister and I usually burst in the door with the question, "What's for dinner?" And no matter what the answer was from the upstairs kitchen, we invariably shot back, "Yuck!" just loud enough for my mother to hear. This would send Mom into a fury. "Why do you *ask* if that is all you ever *say* about it?" or, "Well, that is just too bad, because I am not a short-order cook and there is only one thing for dinner and you will eat it!" or her fallback, "Wait until your father gets home!" This one was powerful because dinner was serious business to Dad. We always ate together and we always ate the same thing as our parents. Even if dinner was spinach meat loaf, broiled salmon, or liver, we got it on our plates. I was a terribly picky eater. I ate rice (with butter) or noodles (also with butter) and candy. Chicken was okay, and so was meat, as long as it didn't taste like liver. (My father would always lie and tell us that we were eating steak when in fact it was occasionally liver.) I ate apples with the skin taken off as my fruit, and carrots and celery as my vegetable group. And that was about it. But tonight I thought it would be best not to fuss at the table and to eat quickly, so I could get to the business at hand.

At dinner my parents would catch up on the day's events. Occasionally my mother would speak in Spanish so that my sister and I would miss anything too juicy. My father could not speak Spanish very well, but they managed to keep many things from us using this method. And since I could now read and spell, the trick of spelling words (". . . so I found out today that Mary, Mary Smith, from the PTA, well, she is having an *a-f-f-a-i-r* with someone from her *o-f-f-i-c-e*") was no longer foolproof. So my sister and I would sit and listen and pretend to understand and then after a while we might resort to fighting to get some of the attention. The problem with getting the attention was that Mom and Dad would notice that I had not eaten whatever was on my plate that I didn't like, and there was always something on my plate that I didn't like. So I had to time the fight just right and deflect attention away from myself if at all possible. Unless the dog was under my seat that night. Sometimes, while my parents were engrossed in the Spanish gossip, I could slip the dog a few morsels without getting caught. It was dangerous, because if I did get caught, there was a good possibility that my parents would reload my plate with more of the dreaded item than I had given to the dog, but it was worth it. The dog did not like vegetables, however, and so he was occasionally useless. In those instances I would try to put my unwanted dinner on my sister's plate. She ate everything, even though she was the worst culprit of the what's-for-dinner-Yuck! exchange each night. She especially loved vegetables, so she came in handy on any Brussels sprout nights.

But tonight everything was going well: baked chicken and rice for dinner, so no problem there. No gossip to distract Mom and Dad and no fighting. Dinner actually went without a hitch. I helped my mom clear and load the dishwasher, and then we settled in the living room for the evening. Evenings usually consisted of doing homework (which meant tears and frustration) or playing games (which also meant tears and frustration). Occasionally we would watch TV. But my mother did not like police shows (too much violence), and we were only allowed to watch one hour a day anyway. So if I had watched *Gilligan's Island* after school then I couldn't even try to con my mother into letting me watch *Mod Squad*, and my sister and I almost always watched *Gilligan's Island*. So we were left with the half-hour comedies to choose from, like *Good Times*, *Maude*, or *The Brady Bunch*.

Before anyone could tell me to get my homework or ask me which game I wanted to play (although "which game to lose" would have been the more accurate question), I announced that I had an important question to ask Mom and Dad. I got them to get rid of my sister by telling them that it was "personal," and while I knew about reproduction by this time, I am sure they were convinced that it was a more-involved "birds and bees" question. Gina was allowed to watch an extra TV show in the den. And I had the floor.

We sat in a little circle, with Mom on the brown leather chair, Dad on the matching ottoman, and me on the carpet.

"So," I said, "what are we?"

Both of my parents had looks of utter confusion on their faces. I had really stumped them. After a pause, my dad asked for clarification.

"You know, what *are* we, what do we believe in?" I asked. "I mean, like, are we Catholic?" I asked the last part hopefully, raising my eyebrows at them and nodding a little as I waited for the answer.

"Well," said my mother, "your father *was* Catholic. But he isn't anymore."

My face fell. "Isn't anymore?" I was confused. "How can you not be something anymore? What are you now, then? What are we now?"

I could tell that I was causing them some kind of discomfort. They glanced at each other and shrugged a little and made tiny grimacing faces, just letting their mouths fall into frowns momentarily.

"Look," I said, wanting to simplify things. This was supposed to have been such an easy question. I was supposed to ask, and they were supposed to say, "Of course, we forgot we're Catholic and we have to go get you the veil first thing tomorrow!" Instead I was sitting here on the itchy yellow and red rug in the living room, staring up at the print of the woman and the moon that hung above my father's head and wondering how to restate the question, to make it easier for them to get it right.

"Look," I repeated, "it's like this: all my friends are

something. Stephanie is a Unitarian, Suzy is Jewish, Michelle is a Catholic, and Lucy is a Presbyterian. So I just want to know, what am I?"

I smiled at them to make them feel better. But I was getting pretty nervous too.

"We're nothing." My father was looking right at me; he had a pleasant, friendly kind of expression. "Nothing," he said again.

"That's right," said my mother. She seemed relieved that Dad had just said it. "Nothing at all. Not any religion. My family is Jewish, of course. But we don't practice Judaism, we don't go to Temple."

She was losing me. How can we be nothing? We have to be something! Everyone is something! I was beginning to get upset. Not only were my dreams of marching down an aisle, dressed in immaculate white with stained glass and candles all around, fading. It was worse, far worse. We were actually nothing. Zero. Not really here. Absent. Not a part of the rest of the world. We were outsiders. Losers. A void.

My parents seemed to think this was somehow amusing. They smiled reassuringly at each other. They nodded their heads at me and said things like, "We like being nothing," and "You don't want to go to church on Sundays, do you?"

"What about God?" I asked as tears streamed down my cheeks.

"Well," the uncomfortable looks returned, "we don't believe in God, either."

I responded with more tears. If God had given me a blood blister for pretending to be sick, what could he do to me if I said I didn't believe in him at all? I feared the wrath of God, and now my parents were telling me they didn't think there was such a person, such a thing. The more they said, the harder I cried. They couldn't make me feel better. Hadn't they been the ones to tell me to watch out or God would get me? No, as I sat there, I realized it had been my friends who had told me that. I was so confused. I felt sick. I was sent to my room. I was told to pull myself together, to stop making so much out of such an unimportant part of our lives, stop overreacting, stop being hysterical. I am sure they finally calmed me down with something to eat, like a bowl of ice cream, and an extra TV show.

So I probably ended the evening with mushy chocolate ice cream, which I liked to make soft by stirring it around for a while before eating it, and watching *Good Times*. Watching another family deal with problems in a light-hearted, joking way may have made me feel better for the moment, but the next day I still felt frightened and uncertain of what to think. I was horrified that we were nothing. I couldn't tell any of my friends. They would probably stop being friends with me if they knew. Who would want to be friends with someone who is nothing?

jesus freaks at the door

my parents both worked. My dad went to work every morning at eight-fifteen and arrived home every evening at five-thirty. There never seemed to be much variation around his arrival and departure times. So if the morning was going badly, well, hold on and ride it out because you know he is out the door in another ten minutes. Or if you have a mess in the living room and you notice that it is five-twenty, well, get cleaning quickly and then you can avoid the yelling about the sloppy living room: "The couch isn't a plaything you know." "Get your shoes out of here!" "Why are there pretzels on the floor?" "Get your dolls off the coffee table."

But my mom worked at a different sort of a job. She left at all kinds of times, and when was she coming home, nobody really knew. She worked for a man who was running for mayor. She helped run his campaign. She went from working one or two days a week for some doctor somewhere to working more than forty hours a week plus weekends. This created some problems in our family. My father hated her job. He hated the hours, the unpredictability of it all, and the weekends on the job. Plus, the whole political business seemed distasteful to him. He did not seem to care that Bill was the good guy, running against the political machine of Mayor Richard Daley. I remember wondering what the heck a political machine was: I imagined something like the mimeograph machine at school, with wheels and sticky ink and cogs and noise. I could not imagine what this machine did, but I knew it was bad. And I knew that Mom had to work like this to get the good guy into City Hall, so that everything could be better for everyone.

We all wore "Bill Singer for Mayor" buttons on our coats. We walked to school chanting, "Singer! Singer! He's our man! Daley belongs in the garbage can!" (We had modified the chant from the last presidential campaign when McGovern had been our man.) We went with Mom to all the marches, rallies, and parades. We even got to ride in the convertible with Bill Singer himself, our future mayor, and we were in one of his TV ads. My mother had walked into my fourth-grade class one day and borrowed me and six of my friends for a few hours. We sat outside (in the freezing cold, but we were told not to *look* cold) and pretended to talk to the candidate. We would nod our heads and try to look thoughtful, then we would stop and were told to smile, and we would do that for a while. We returned to school in time for lunch, and a few weeks later we saw ourselves on TV.

The results of my mother having this job were that my parents fought all the time (rather, all the time that they were both home), my dad started to cook (both because my mom was out and because after his trip to Italy he was interested in cooking), and my sister and I were home alone for long stretches of time. I was the classic latchkey child. I literally wore the house key on a string around my neck. Every day I

was the one who opened the side door to our house for me
and my sister and, occasionally, a friend or two. Sometimes
I would take the key off during gym class and forget to put
it back on, especially when we were doing any work on the
uneven parallel bars. If I didn't take the key off from around
my neck, it would swing down and hit me in the face, usually causing me to do so badly during my turn that the gym
teacher would yell at me and I would spend the rest of the
forty-five minutes trying not to cry because if you cried in
front of Mr. Wrickrack he called you a sissy. If I did take it
off and forget it, then I had to walk all the way back to
school to get it from the doorknob in the gym, and Gina
would be mad at me for making her walk back to school, and
she would be hungry, and she would cry because the
crossing lady would be gone from Lincoln Avenue and we
would have to cross the scary-busy street by ourselves.

Once we got home we could have a snack and we could
watch TV. The hour-a-day rule was gone by the time my
mother started working long hours . . . or at least there was
no enforcement of it. A few days a week some babysitter
would come to stay with us, but it took a while to get to our
house from the Catholic high school she attended, so we
always got home first. By the time the sitter arrived, we were
in front of the TV eating some ghastly food that we had
found, like sugar cubes, or a bowl of peanut butter with
semisweet chocolate squares chopped up and sprinkled on
top, or confectioners' sugar mixed with milk to make a
"frosting," which we dyed pink, or my sister's favorite, egg
whites beaten until stiff with sugar and food coloring and
eaten uncooked. My mother did not have any junk food in
the house. We were supposed to eat fruit or wheat crackers

or occasionally oatmeal cookies. No potato chips, no cakes, no ice cream, or candy was to be consumed. So we scrounged for anything we could find that might satisfy our need for sugar, or anything that even closely resembled junk food. Then we would watch horrible afternoon TV and do our homework during the commercials.

During any kind of school holiday or day off, my sister and I would be largely on our own. Summers we went to camp, but before and after camp, we would stay home and watch TV for what seemed like days on end. We would call my mother on the phone six or seven times a day, to have her settle a fight, to answer a question (usually a question that was actually part of a fight), to ask her what we were supposed to eat for lunch, or to find out what was for dinner.

One day in the spring, I was the only one at home. My sister was at Lizzie's house across the street. I was most likely in a fight with Lizzie's sister, Linda, which would explain why I was not across the street as well. I was in a fight with Linda every other day or so, and the fights only lasted a few hours. So I was probably home on this particular morning to wait out the few hours needed before Linda and I would resume our dolls or dress-up or whatever other game we were in the middle of when the fight broke out. The TV was on, but the light was bright in the room and the screen was hard to see. I was definitely bored. Later in the day, I was going to go to my mother's office. I was going to take the bus with my sister to get there, which I had done before, so I knew what number bus to take (the number thirty-six) and where to get off (Wacker Drive).

So I was not really watching TV as I pulled on some socks and changed from my nightshirt into my yellow *Tour de France* T-shirt when the doorbell rang. Only it was the front door. We always used the side door, and everyone we knew used the side door, too. But sometimes a new mailman or a deliveryman would ring the front bell, so I went down the stairs to answer it.

It was hard to get the front door opened because it was so rarely used. The lock was sticky, and the door itself was hard to pull open. The glass in the door rattled as I tugged at it, and I finally got it opened with a big pull. The air was cool—there was still a winter feeling this early in the spring—and I immediately wished I had put shoes on. My socks were not enough to keep the chill away from my toes. It was really bright out there, so my eyes took a minute to adjust. I blinked and saw that there were two people at our front door—a man and a woman. They were well dressed, or they seemed normal looking in any case. They had darkish skin, like they were from Puerto Rico or Mexico, and dark hair.

"Good morning, little girl," the man said. He did have a slight Spanish accent. "We were wondering if your parents were at home today."

"No," I answered, feeling a bit suspicious. "They are both at work."

I was a little worried about telling them this fact, although I was not sure what else to say. It was clear that I was home alone, and I wasn't a fast enough thinker to get a lie together in five seconds.

"Oh, I see," said the man. "We are your neighbors. We live over there." He gestured to behind our house. I knew that there was a neighborhood with Spanish-speaking people back there, so I assumed that was where they had come from.

"Oh," I said. I was unsure of what they wanted.

"Well," he said, "we just wanted to know, what is your relationship to Jesus Christ, our Lord and Savior? Do you know him? Do you want to share in his love?"

"Oh, umm," I hesitated. I smiled a little in confusion as I thought of how to answer the questions. I knew about Jesus—Michelle had told me about him being the son of God and then dying on a cross—but I didn't want to love him. My parents didn't seem to want to know anything about him: why would they want to love the son of God when they didn't even believe in God? But I could not tell these people that we were nothing and that they were wasting their time with our household. I didn't want to seem like a bad person, like someone who wouldn't want to know Jesus. And besides, maybe they had the answer I had been waiting for. Maybe these people had some information that could help me. They were smiling back at me, waiting for me to say something.

"Well," I said, finally, "we don't go to church." I figured this was safe. It didn't mean we were nonbelievers; maybe we were just lazy.

They shook their heads and looked sad. "You don't go to church?" They seemed confused. "How will you know God— how will you come to love Jesus—if you don't go to church? You must tell your parents that you want to go to church . . . what is your name?"

"Nica," I answered before thinking. They didn't seem like they wanted to hurt me. They might even be trying to help me. I thought it would be okay for them to know my name.

"Nica, we want to talk to your parents about taking you

to church," they said. "It is very important that you come to church. We will give you these books for you to show your parents and we will call you to see if they are interested in taking you to our church."

They handed me some colorful booklets. They had light, watery pictures on them: a sunset, a field, some sheep, a bearded man.

"Thank you." I felt unsure of what to do. I was pretty sure I knew that my parents wouldn't want to go to church or talk about going to church. I was pretty sure they wouldn't want to read the booklets, either.

"I am Carlos and this is Maria," the man said. "We want to talk to you and to your parents about our church, so can we have your phone number? Then we can call and find out how you liked the books we gave you."

They both seemed so nice. They really cared about what I thought about the books; they wanted to call me to talk to me. That didn't seem bad; that actually seemed nice. So I gave them my phone number. I wrote it for them on a paper they had.

"Thanks," they said. "Enjoy the books and we will call." They smiled and waved at me as they walked down the front steps and went along the sidewalk to another house. I knew that our neighbors were not at home, but I decided not to tell my new friends not to bother, since I didn't want to seem rude.

The sun was very bright on the front steps, and it was going to be a warm day. I was feeling quite adult, like I had done the right thing. I had been polite to people who had come to the door. I had behaved properly. I was not sure about giving them my name and phone number, but, well, what harm could come from that after all? They weren't bad guys, thieves, or murderers. I was sure of that. They hadn't even asked for money. They were only trying to help. I shut the door and stood in the unused front hall for a moment. It was warm in there with the sun coming through the glass panels in the door and above it.

The front hall had a funny smell. It didn't smell like our house. It smelled old and dusty. The wallpaper was from before we owned the house, and the stairs were old, too. They had peeling linoleum on them. This front entrance was on my dad's list of things to do around the house. He was going to repaper it, or paint it, and redo the stairs. Maybe we would even use it one day, as a more formal entrance to the house, since it led right up into our living room. I turned and started up the stairs, and with each step I began to feel that giving out my phone number had not been such a smart idea. By the middle of the staircase I was feeling shaky and scared. By the time I was at the top, in front of the bar my father had built into a closet, I was sure I had made a very bad decision. As I breathed the bourbon-scented air that came from the bar, as I stood at the top of the stairs frozen with doubt and fear, I realized that I had broken all the rules of answering the door. I had forgotten to ask who it was before opening the door. I had told the people that I was home alone, rather than lying. Wasn't I supposed to tell anyone asking that my mom was in the shower, or that my dad was in the backyard, or some lie like that? Yes, I was. I wasn't to tell anyone that my parents were at work, gone all day. Even if it wasn't the truth, it was a lie to protect me, so it was okay. And my name, I had told them my name. And worse than all of that, I had given them my phone number.

If these people, these strangers, had my name, my address, and my phone number, then surely that meant they could come and get me! I still had the booklets in my hand. I walked the few steps from the bar to the living room and I sat down with a thud in front of the TV.

I felt like I'd been punched in my stomach—the lurching and flipping feeling—as I realized that far from doing the right thing, I had actually done the wrong thing. I had done the total opposite of the right thing. I had given out my name and my phone number. I might as well have put my head in a lion's mouth. Wow, the depths of my stupidity amazed me. I was not fit to be home alone, to be in charge, to have any responsibilities. As soon as I had come across a challenge, boom, I had fallen prey to my own inexperience, to my lack of quick thinking, to my stupidity. I sat in front of the TV for a long time. My show had ended and a soap opera had come on. I was so engrossed in my own plight that I was actually watching a dreaded soap opera.

Well, I finally figured, no one would know about it. I was here alone. How could anyone ever know? Maybe I could answer the phone every time it rings for the next year. That way, if the people call I can tell them to go away, or that my mother is in the shower, or whatever I was supposed to have said this morning on my front porch. No one would ever know that I had given out my phone number to total strangers.

I turned off the TV and went to finish getting dressed to go to my mother's office. I hid the booklets in my top drawer. I would try to forget about the whole thing.

I thought about getting to my mom's office. If I was really lucky and I got there in time I would be allowed to answer the phone calls coming into the campaign headquarters. They had a switchboard, just like on the old TV shows, and I got to connect the callers to the proper phone in the office by plugging the cords into the holes on the board in front of me. I loved working the switchboard. I had only made one mistake, when I pulled out the wrong plug and disconnected Margaret, a woman who worked on the campaign with my mom. There was some trouble over that and some concern that I was too young to be handling the switchboard, but if the receptionist was at lunch and I was in the office, all agreed that it was better than one of the real workers taking the time to do it.

I called over to the Allen's house to tell Gina to get home so that we could go, but she wanted to stay. After some phone calls between my mother and Mrs. Allen, we got it settled that Gina would stay at Lizzie's while I would go to Mom's office alone.

That was fine with me. I didn't relish the idea of having Gina along. I had to watch out for her on the bus and across the streets. Then, once at the office she would get all the attention. Sometimes more than I got, because she was so cute.

"Fine, let her stay at the Allen's," I thought as I put on my Buster Brown saddle shoes and put the key around my neck. I had the bus fare in my pocket and I headed toward the bus stop on Halstad Street feeling a mix of relief to be out of the house so no more people of Christ could get me and of dread at what my mom would say if she found out what I had done.

When I got to the office, there was no time for the switchboard. My mother wanted to go get lunch and then stop at Marshall Field's for something, so out we went. We were alone in the elevator, and for some reason, without thinking (because I really had not intended to tell her, so I could not have been thinking), I told her what had happened that morning. I told her about the people and the questions and the booklets. I even told her about the phone number. As I told her, she widened her eyes, her chin went up, and she began to look dismayed.

As the elevator descended, it felt as if it got smaller and smaller with each floor. In my mind, it was in miniature by the time we reached the lobby. I didn't cry, although I felt I was about to. I wasn't really punished, but my mother scolded me and reminded me in harsh tones about the conduct she expected of me when I was home alone. In fact, she told me not to go to the front door anymore. She may have threatened to hire a babysitter if I did this kind of thing again. In the end, though, she told me not to worry, that these people would probably never call and that, most likely, they were harmless.

This brought me little comfort. Not only had I broken a cardinal, staying-home-alone rule, I had also let religion into the house. Somehow—and I don't know how exactly, but somehow—it was made clear that those kinds of people are not okay. People who want to talk to you about God, those religious "Jesus Freaks" (as my father would later call them), were just not okay. It was not a good idea to talk to them. They could somehow "get" you if you listened to them for too long.

Some time after the "Jesus Freaks" came to the door, I was in the park with my friend Stephanie. Some other Christians wanted to speak with us about our relationships to

Jesus and God the Father. I scowled at them and hissed that I wasn't interested. I was sure at the very least they would get me to give up some vital piece of personal information that would cause me more heartache and embarrassment. Stephanie, on the other hand, was perfectly happy to enter into a discussion with these crazed people. She even went so far as to tell them that she was half-Jewish. Horrified at her admission and sure that some ill would come of it, I pulled her along. I had to get away from those people, that was for sure. Stephanie viewed it as a sport, a-get-into-a-fight-with-the-Jesus-Freaks-for-points debate. But I did not want to debate what I was so unsure about. It was better to leave it alone; no questions meant no answers. And the answers I had gotten so far were not what I wanted to hear. So I stopped asking and stopped talking about it. Religion was already a topic I had learned to avoid.

chapter 4

don't tell
(about the jesus freaks
at the door)

Somehow I decided that the worst thing—the thing that could never happen, the thing that would ruin my whole life—would be if anyone found out about my "new friends," the Jesus Freaks. I could live with my mom knowing; her reaction had been what I expected. She was dismayed with my mistake of opening the door and divulging personal information to strangers, but she was not permanently angry. I could deal with my dad knowing and I knew my mom would tell him. They always talked about us and knew everything as one unit. But no one could know beyond those two. Especially my sister, who was like a representative of everyone else. She definitely could not be in on this "secret."

For months, my father held the secret of the incident at the front door over my head. If I wouldn't do my homework, if I did not like what was on my plate, if I misbehaved at all in any way, he played the "I'll tell" card.

It was obvious to Gina that there was something to be found out. And that worked right into my father's plan. He could torture me with the threat of telling the secret and he could torture Gina by not telling her. Sometimes I would join in on the taunting of my sister, "I have a secret and I'm not telling!" And other times Gina would act as if she knew. "Dad told me," she would lie, "and now I'm telling everyone!" I would more than likely beat her up when she threatened this, then Mom or Dad would get involved, and the cycle would renew itself. The secret ruled my life one way or the other. I could not seem to get away from it. The truth was that I had done a stupid thing, and if anyone found out they would see how stupid I really was.

I tried to prove that I was not stupid by doing well in school. I was in fourth grade with Miss Crews as my teacher. I was in a class with my old friends Michelle, Stephanie, Mary Beth, and Ted (I had been in the same class as some of them since kindergarten). Tom sat next to me, but he was the worst kid in school (he had also been in my class since kindergarten and had established a bad reputation early). He bullied everyone on the schoolyard, he took the weaker kids' snack money, and he and his thug friends once took my mittens on a cold Chicago winter day. Tom was so bad that he would look up Miss Crews's skirt when she walked up and down the aisles correcting papers or helping us with our studies. She was tall and quite thin and she wore tiny miniskirts although she was not particularly young. Tom would put his head down on his desk and peek right up her skirt as she would bend over a desk, usually mine, since he was in close proximity to me. After she was gone, he would giggle and whisper to me that she was not wearing any underwear. This was so intriguing that I had to see for myself. I followed Tom's lead and had myself a look the next time she bent over a nearby desk. It seemed to be true; there was no sign of any underwear. I was horrified by the whole thing and I told on Tom the next day when he dropped his pencil to get a better look. Miss Crews seemed confused by what I was telling her, then she turned a dark red, swallowed hard, and thanked me for my tattling.

Miss Crews was loony and really, truly nuts. She loved Stephanie and me and gave us candy every day, especially after I told her about Tom. Our moms were on the PTA, and so Miss Crews seemed to be sucking up to us. She would give us the candy and ask us, "How's Mommy?" with a strange smile on her face. There was something conspiratorial about her. She would narrow her eyes and wait for our answer. It was as if she was expecting some dirt, some tidbit to use against our moms at the next PTA meeting. Stephanie and I were just happy for the candy, and we always answered in unison, "She's fine." I am sure we disappointed Miss Crews constantly with our lack of information, but she never showed it. And she always offered us candy the next day. Was she trying to wear us down, build our trust, or get us hooked on the sugar so that some day she could really get us? In truth, she was just mentally unstable.

The schoolwork was not very challenging for me in fourth grade, except for math. "New math" was introduced and threw most of us for a loop. I couldn't do old math, and new math seemed to require a firm understanding of how old math worked. All those days of staring out the window during third-grade math were haunting me. There was hardly a math period in third grade that I could recall. I was too busy looking at the trees and the sky and dreaming of me and Ted off on a fairy-tale adventure and married happily ever after.

Fourth grade was the year of multiplication. That was a big hurdle for me. I didn't like to memorize the tables given to me, I just did not want to do it. After I got a near-failing grade in the middle of the year, my father took the matter into his hands. I had almost failed third-grade math, and there was no way he was going to let me fail fourth-grade math. He was an electrical engineer and used math every day. He knew it was important and told me that I would never get anywhere in life if I couldn't do simple math. Simple math was just about killing me: simple math was an oxymoron.

Each night after dinner, I would sit across from my father at the kitchen table and he would drill me on my multiplication tables. I had gotten a multiplication table "toy" for Christmas. It was a square grid with the times tables in rows (1×1, 1×2, 1×3, and so on, along the top row, and going down, all the tables went along with the nine times tables along the last row). To find the answer to the problem you pushed the little button down and the number was on the side of the tile above. It was very low-tech, so nothing lit up and no song played if you answered correctly. It was a horrid present, and I got two of them; the green one was for multiplication tables, the blue one for division.

I sat with the green box on my lap as my dad quizzed me. The sevens and the nines were the worst, and we seemed to spend hours on those. "Seven times four!" he would boom at me. I would sit immobile. It was the fifth time we had done the seven times table, and I still did not have the answer. My finger tapped the grid; maybe I could push it down quickly when he blinked. No, that would never work. I was desperate. He was waiting. Tears slid out of my eyes and his face became hard.

"Crying won't do you any good!" he roared. "You are sitting here until you know this. Hell, Nica, this is easy. I can't believe you are in fourth grade and this is so hard for you." I sat still and tears continued to drip down my face.

"The answer is twenty-eight." His voice was calm, but there was the possibility of him blowing up at any moment.

"It is the same as four times seven. Now go to your room and study these tables until bedtime." And his hand came down hard on the table top as I slid out of my seat. Wham!

"And stop crying, for God's sake!" he yelled after me.

Once in my room, I would cry for a few minutes and then recover and read or write in my journal. Writing in my journal was fun. It was a tiny book. It was yellow with a picture of a flower on the front and a tiny lock with a tiny key. The lock was worthless, though. My sister could get it opened without the key and did so often. She would occasionally add a word or thought on a page, so I knew she had been there. Anyway, I would rarely look at my times tables after I was out of the kitchen and away from Dad. And the next time we sat down for the drill, it would go pretty much the same way. Sometimes he would get mad faster. Other times he would just send me away after one or two wrong answers. I did eventually learn those tables. But the nines and the sevens still give me a lot of problems.

One day we came to school to find Miss Crews gone. Gone for good, it turned out. She had suffered a nervous breakdown and, according to my mother, "had been taken out of the school in a straitjacket." I had no idea what a nervous breakdown was and I did not have a clue what a straitjacket was, either. But it sounded dramatic. So I told everyone what my mother had said. My friends and I imagined that a nervous breakdown was some kind of major fit, something like what our little sisters might have, but as a grown-up. And a straitjacket! Whatever it was, it sounded bad. Miss Crews was sick, we were told by the sweet old principal. We nodded our heads solemnly but knew that it was not a normal kind of sick.

For the rest of fourth grade, we had a substitute named

Miss Cass. She had long blonde hair. She was young and pretty. I liked her immediately and came to love her, since she never taught us anything. She just read us books. She read us book after book out loud. My favorite was the *Last of the Really Great Whangdoodles*. The children in the book travel to another world, and I always loved books with other worlds. The possibility that I might someday escape from my life was exciting and I never failed to push to the back of a closet or tap on a mirror in hopes of finding Narnia or Oz on the other side. Miss Cass read us tons more books as well. I don't really recall any other classwork from fourth grade. But I remember having a good time.

The Jesus-Freaks-at-the-front-door secret still hung over me the rest of that year and through the summer. Finally, one day as my father was using it to get me and my sister into fits, I told her what the secret was. I just told her. There. Done. No more secret. You know what she did? She burst out laughing.

"That is *it*?" she hooted. "That is the big, bad secret? That you gave our phone number to someone? Jeeze Louise, Nica! Who cares!"

And that was that. I still had no idea what to do about our family's religious status, but at least I was not keeping a deep, dark secret anymore. I may have given out my phone number, but I hadn't ever heard from the people who had wanted to help me know God; I had not gotten any of my questions about religion answered. I had instead reinforced the idea that religion caused problems, made me feel inadequate for not being part of it, and made me feel stupid for even trying to get it.

chapter 5

i believe in mary worth

it was becoming obvious, with the question I asked my parents and the meeting with the Jesus Freaks at my door, that I was curious. I was curious about what my friends did on the weekend days they spent in religious institutions. I heard them speak of church or temple, with the cookies afterward, the playrooms, and the Sunday school teachers. I thought it sounded fun, and even though I didn't belong, I thought it might be exciting to try. Maybe if I went with my friends and followed what they did, maybe then I would understand.

Then one weekend I had a Saturday night sleepover with Stephanie. We woke up on Sunday morning to a large breakfast at the dining room table. After that it was off to church.

Breakfast was horrifying, with eggs, bacon, and fruit. I hated them all. Stephanie's mom was not one to hear the words "no, thank you" even if you did muster the courage to utter them. She was a doctor from South America who was formal and strict. I addressed her as Dr. Sawyer, even after I had been at Stephanie's house one hundred times. Dr. Sawyer was small and intense. There was no room for silliness, so neatness and manners were always required. And eating was a given. They were a family who ate formally at the dining room table, and everyone had to eat what was put on her plate. That was not so foreign to me, but the Sawyer family did not have a dog to "help out" with unwanted dinner, so I was terrified at Stephanie's dinner table. If I was lucky, really lucky, Dr. Sawyer would make her potato gnocchi for dinner. She was from Argentina, but her ancestors were Italian. Those gnocchi were the best thing I had ever tasted. But breakfast was another story. I somehow gagged down my eggs (scrambled eggs were palatable, but these were fried) and picked at my fruit. If I took long enough, Dr. Sawyer would give up because she did not want to be late. So when it was time to leave for church, I cleared my plate with Stephanie and she quickly scraped the uneaten fruit into the garbage disposal.

As we piled into the Sawyer's car, I commented on the fact that I had never been to church. I hoped that it would be okay with my parents that I was tagging along. Dr. Sawyer looked at me in the rearview mirror.

"Never been to church?" she asked. "What is your family?"

I told her that we were Jewish, because of my mother, but that really we were not anything. I said "not anything" to avoid the word "nothing." "Not anything" sounded less finite and less awful.

"Stephanie's father is Jewish," Dr. Sawyer said. And she muttered "bastard" under her breath as she pulled out of the driveway.

Stephanie had two doctors in her family, and when her mother later remarried, she had three. Dr. Sawyer (Mr.) lived in the suburbs with his second wife, Barb. Barb had been Dr. Sawyer's nurse and now she was his wife. Even I could figure that one out. They had a great apartment in a high-rise outside the city. Stephanie had invited me to sleep over at her dad's once, and it had been a gas. He picked me up in his car without a top. We went to a toy store, and he bought us cool toys and also let us eat junk food. We had cheese fondue for dinner and then chocolate fondue for dessert. We even had marshmallows to dip in the chocolate. I was in heaven.

Dr. Sawyer (Mrs.) was popular with my mother because she was a real "liberated" woman. She was a working mother and a doctor, no less. Plus, she would not let the old-fashioned principal of our school call her *Mrs.* Sawyer. The principal complained that it was too confusing to have two Dr. Sawyers in the family, so she said she would just call the mother Mrs. Sawyer and the father would have the "Doctor" title. Stephanie's mother would have none of it. "Why don't you call him Mr. Sawyer, and call me Doctor!" she was reported to have said in her strong Spanish accent.

Stephanie was "mixed" like me: one parent was Jewish and the other Christian, but she seemed to *be* something, maybe even two things. As we drove to the church, I was worried that I would not be allowed to be there, since I was not religious. Would there be some kind of test they would give me? Stephanie had said that we only had to stay for part of the service, but I had no idea what a service was. I hoped it would not be anything too terrible and I hoped I would not have to say anything. Maybe it would be like when a teacher called on me at school when I was not prepared. Maybe I would be embarrassed in front of Dr. Sawyer and all the other people. I started to think that coming to church had not been such a great idea.

We pulled up to a nice-looking church called the Unitarian Church of Greater Chicago. We went inside, where there were colorful windows and lots of blond wood. The room seemed like an auditorium to me except for the seats; they were long rows of wooden benches. Everyone seemed nice enough, greeting one another and asking how the week had been. We sat in a row in the back and the service began. It turned out that the service was like a lecture: a man stood up in front of the room and talked for quite a long time. He talked about a lot of things and kept mentioning God. There was no mention of "knowing Jesus," like I heard from those people who came to my door. Jesus didn't even come up much. None of it made much sense to me, but at least I was not being tested or called on. I ended up feeling bored more than anything else, and I wanted the service to end. I was hungry, since I had not eaten my breakfast, and I found myself thinking about the cookies. I hoped they would be good, not oatmeal or healthy; maybe they would be Oreos. I was also sleepy, since Stephanie and I had stayed up until past midnight (after all, what was a sleepover if you actually went to sleep?) and I knew that Dr. Sawyer would be furious if she saw me nodding off, so I kept my eyes opened wide. When the talking was over, there was some singing, and then we were allowed to leave for Sunday school. It was not very formal, and we mostly stood in a room that looked like a study and talked to Stephanie's older sister and her friends. Then we ran up and down one of the hallways, playing a silent game of tag so that we were undetected by Dr. Sawyer. When the service ended and the grown-ups came out, there were some cookies, but Dr. Sawyer gave us the just-take-one look. So the cookies were not such a great thing in the end.

At least I had been to church. It wasn't as if I felt different after going there; I felt the same, with no answers having been offered to me about my own status. If that was all there was, talking, singing, and no-so-great-cookies, then I could live without it. But I wanted to see some other ways to be religious, too. So I arranged other sleepovers with other friends and went to their churches or synagogues.

I felt more comfortable at Suzy's temple than I did at Stephanie's church, but that may have been because I was terrified of Dr. Sawyer. But Suzy's mom was a dream mom, like something out of a TV show. The kids went straight to Saturday school, so there was no long talking part, and there were cookies right there when we walked in. Mrs. Leland would never give us the just-take-one look, so we got to have quite a few of those temple cookies.

I liked the Saturday school, too. Suzy introduced me to the class, and everyone said, "Shalom," which is the Jewish word for hello. Then we colored in some candelabra and spinning tops, since it was November and close to Chanukah. I learned that Chanukah is the celebration of light, that the oil in the temple was supposed to last for one night, but instead it lasted for eight. It was a miracle! So that was why Suzy got eight presents and why there were eight candles on the candelabra (which had its own special name, a menorah), one for each night that the oil lasted. At the end of the class the teacher had an announcement. She said, "Okay, everyone. Have a nice week and remember, let's see fewer Christmas trees and more Chanukah bushes this year!!" I thought that was funny. Jews could have trees and call them "bushes" and they could decorate them and put the presents under them, just like at Christmas. So maybe our

Christmas tree could be a Chanukah bush this year. I had made an ornament at the Saturday school out of the drawing of the spinning top, with glitter and blue paint. I would hang that on the tree and see how it looked.

I went to a few other church services, but I don't recall having much connection with anything that happened there. Mostly it seemed that there was the service part, with the windows and the benches and the guy who talked and talked followed by the part when the kids were allowed to leave. There was always Sunday school, but it seemed that we mostly went to the gym or the rec room or just roamed around the hallways. I wasn't feeling like I was something after going to church, so it didn't seem to me that our family was missing much by being nothing. So I stopped going to my friends' churches. I had had enough of that little exploration.

I did, however, enter a church regularly around that same time. Girl Scout meetings were held each week in a church building near school (I had graduated from Brownies). It was a corner church, a brownish-red building with nice windows and big wooden doors. It was the same church where we had held pretend school during the teacher's strike when I was in first grade. After a week of not having school, a bunch of mothers got together and taught us in that same church. I remember my mom reading us a book about the name *Chicago*, how it was an Indian name that meant "wild onions" or "roaming buffalo" or "waving grasses." This was before the term *Native American*, so we learned about "Indians." Even though I liked studying teepees, squaws, and braves, I was not so happy about being taught by my mother. I was sweaty, it was crowded, and while my mother was reading she was giving me the fish eye because I was squirming around the carpet with my other little first-grade pals. I was happy once "school" was over and we could play in the big gym next to the church. I was even happier once the strike was settled and we didn't have to picket the school with Mom or be taught by her.

Now I was in the church again as a Girl Scout. The only two things I liked about Girl Scouts were the uniform and the *Girl Scout Handbook*. My uniform was a hand-me-down from my older cousin Lisa, and it was green and had a sash to wear across the top. The sash, of course, was for sewing all the badges onto, but we never seemed to earn any badges. I don't know where I got the *Girl Scout Handbook*, but I loved it. I read it over and over, imagining all the badges I would earn, all the terrific, heroic, fabulous things I would do like hike in the mountains, build a real campfire, sew a dress, cook, and help at the old folks home. But all our Girl Scout troop seemed to do was eat snacks and do art projects. Sometimes we would make the snacks, but it never required any real cooking. It was things like "no-bakes" or things to eat that were assembled from existing foods. The art projects we did were fun, but they were not the elaborate, wonderful projects from my book. They were gluing eyes on a cardboard spider and making egg-carton caterpillars, things I had done in school years before.

My Girl Scout troop never went on trips, either. I had been camping with my family plenty of times. I didn't love it, but it was kind of neat to sleep in a tent and have a campfire. I thought that it might be really fun if it was with a bunch of other girls. Plus, I dreamed of the s'mores that the Girl Scouts had made famous. My mother had told us about

them, and we had gotten them once during a family campout. But I wanted to eat them on a Girl Scout campout, like
in the *Handbook*. I thought we could all earn the camping
badges by doing all the camping things perfectly. But the
only "campout" we had was held at the church. We were
going to sleep at the church. We brought our sleeping bags,
as if we were really camping out, but we unrolled them in a
living room in the church building. I was very excited to
have a Girl Scout sleepover, even if it was not held in a
wooded glen with owls hooting and a campfire (which we
had built perfectly) glowing. Apparently we were going to
make s'mores anyway, using the church oven somehow.

The evening was pleasant until it got dark. Then the
whole church got creepy and creaky. The rooms were poorly
lit, and the hallways had only dim bulbs in them. Suddenly
I noticed all the statues and paintings of Bible scenes. They
had a sinister, foreboding sense in the gloom. Going down to
the basement kitchen was terrifying. I don't remember the
s'mores at all, either because we were too scared to make
them or we did make them but I don't recall, because all I
remember is fear. Also absent from my memories of that
night is an adult. I know we had a troop leader and I imagine
she was present in the church with all of us, but I have no
recollection of a safe, calm adult being anywhere near the
group of us. The group consisted of four or five girls my age,
plus one or two who were slightly older. It is the older girls
that I remember most clearly. This is because they tortured
me. They preyed on the scared and the weak. That was me;
the other little girls might have been frightened by them and
the stories they told, but I was terrified.

They sat us on our sleeping bags and told us ghost stories, standard fare I am sure. But in that large, old, dark church, the stories were vivid, and it seemed very likely that something terrible would happen to me at any minute. The one I remember was the story of Mary Worth. Mary Worth lives in the mirror. Before she got put in the mirror, she was very beautiful and had long black hair. Something bad happened to Mary, and she lost her beauty and retreated (or was put by a spell) into the mirror. She hates anyone to see her, since she is no longer beautiful, so if you catch a glimpse of her in a mirror she will rip your eyes out with her long, sharp, red nails. The way to see her is to turn out the lights in the bathroom, or in any room with a mirror, and say, "I believe in Mary Worth!" three times, followed by "I hate Mary Worth!" three times. Upon hearing these words she will come out of the mirror and do that nasty eye-ripping trick, and then you'll be blind forever and miserable because she will scratch your eyes out and that will hurt for a long time and might never heal. In fact, you might live the rest of your life with bloody, empty eye sockets.

Needless to say, I did not sleep after that. It seemed that I finally had something to believe in: the wrath of Mary Worth. It sounded just as bad as the wrath of God, since he could make you blind too. Every time I closed my eyes, I was sure that Mary Worth would sneak into the room and get me because there were mirrors all around the church building like in the bathrooms and above the fireplaces. She could get into the building if she wanted to, since the other girls had uttered the words, the words to conjure her. I fell asleep eventually, with my head buried in my sleeping bag and under my pillow. I woke up sweaty, sticky from my own hot breath, and extremely relieved that my parents were picking me up for our Sunday breakfast at the Pancake House.

As soon as I got home, I removed all the mirrors from my bedroom. My Aunt Jean had given me a little white mirror with a drawer for jewelry to set on my dresser, and I loved it. The mirror could swivel up and down so I could see myself in different light; it was glamorous and made me feel grown-up. But out it went. That mirror was sure death. And I never, *ever* walked into a dark bathroom. I turned the light on first and waited outside to make sure Mary Worth was not in the room. I knew I was safe in the light because she never appeared when the lights were on. She didn't want to see herself, since she was so hideous.

I never went back into that church again. I never went back to Girl Scouts, either. I never earned a badge and never made real, official Girl Scout s'mores by a real girl-made campfire. My parents had never been crazy about the Girl Scout thing. Even though my mother had been a Girl Scout, she found it a bit sexist for the newly enlightened "age of feminism." They thought that the sleepover at the church was a dumb idea in the first place; "real scouts go camping" is what they said. When I came back from the overnight terrified of mirrors, they just rolled their eyes at me and told me not to be ridiculous. "There is no one living in a mirror," they sighed. So it didn't matter to them if I quit Girl Scouts. They signed me up for swimming and pottery instead.

Once when the Boy Scout recruiter came to speak to my class, I boldly raised my hand and inquired about girls joining up. He told me, with a wry grin, to go check out the Girl Scouts. That would be fine, I answered, if all I want to do is cook things that don't need cooking or glue eyes onto egg cartons. I challenged him to show us where in the *Boy Scout Manual* it said "No Girls" and I would have kept it up had my teacher not interceded and told me to be quiet. I don't know what took hold of me that day the man from the Boy Scouts came. I didn't even like camping; I just hated that the boys got to do cool, adventuresome things and the girls got to sleep in a creepy church and had the life scared out of them.

chapter 6

the dead bird

i̇t was a cold spring day. We had lots of those in
Chicago. It would be cold for months when it was supposed to be spring. Easter was often celebrated during a
snowstorm or on a day more reminiscent of Thanksgiving
than what a spring festival of rebirth and new growth
should be. On this day I was home from school early. And
I was alone. Perhaps it was a half day. Perhaps my sister
was at a friend's house. Perhaps I was to have gone somewhere and then changed my mind. For some reason,
instead of entering the house with my key on the shoe-
string, I went into the backyard. Sometimes there were
patches of ice big enough to slide around on, not with ice
skates but just in boots or oxford shoes. Maybe I went back
there to do that for a while. Maybe the dog had been put
out and I went around back to get him. I am not sure how
I got into the backyard, but there I was.

We had a big yard. One half of it was concrete patio.
There was a large picnic table where we seemed to spend
most of the summer, and we had a rectangular gravel-filled
box. It was like a sandbox, only with gravel instead of sand.
At one time we had a red and white dome in the box, on top

of the gravel, and it had rope and wood swings inside. But it had been dismantled when it had started to rust.

There was a huge elm tree on one side of the patio with the picnic table under it. The tree was truly enormous; the trunk was so large even my father could not get his arms around it. It had carpenter ants living in it. My father routinely put a sticky brown paste around the trunk and base of the tree to kill the ants. The carpenter ants were black, fat, and nasty. We stomped on them violently when we saw them. They would kill our tree, and we didn't want it to die. Then we would have no place for the hammock.

The hammock was my favorite part of the backyard. My parents had bought it in Cozumel, Mexico, and it was a soft, woven cocoon all summer long. We played "mummy rises" for hours in the hammock. Gina or I would go inside and wrap up in the hammock. The other would give ten pushes, after which the "mummy" would unwrap and sit up, as slowly and creepily as possible. We would make appropriate spooky noises until the person playing the mummy stopped swinging. Then it was the next person's turn. It wasn't a complicated game, but we loved it.

The second half of our backyard was the garden. We had a square patch of grass in the middle that my father was forever mowing with a manual push mower. He was also forever yelling at us to get off the grass, since he had either just watered it, just fed it, or we were just plain going to kill it. We had flower beds and trees around the grass. We had an olive tree, a plum tree, a crab apple tree, and a mulberry tree. The crab apples were awful; I had tried one on a dare from my sister. I never saw a plum or an olive, but there were lots of mulberries, which my sister ate but I refused; they were slimy and bitter.

I opened the black chain link gate and went into the backyard on this particular day. There was no one around. The picnic table was under the tree, but the hammock was not yet hung on the hook, and no toys or balls were outside either. It was so quiet I could hear myself breathing. I was wearing my winter coat. It was a gray-blue plaid, with some rust color woven in. I had liked it at the beginning of the winter, but I was sick of it now. It tied with a sash, which I tightened to warm me up, and I glanced around the yard.

Lying on the ground there was a still brown bird. It was perfect, and perfectly still. I could see its eyes, its beak, and each beautiful feather. There was a bit of white under the beak, and the wings had gray and brown in them. The bird did not show signs of being harmed. It did not look mauled or maimed, just silent and stiff.

I bent down and gently touched it. Maybe it was just asleep and I could wake it up, then it would happily fly off to its family, to its friends, to its nest. I stroked the feathers, I nudged the little body, but nothing happened. I touched its tiny head and beak, and even moved it an inch or two, but it didn't wake up. It was dead. Really and truly dead.

I had been crouching over the dead bird for a while, and my legs were getting that prickly feeling, so I stood up. My head was a little dizzy when I stood up, so I must have gotten up too fast. I looked down at the bird again . . . poor little thing. I felt so sad that I started to cry. Tears came slowly at first, then flowed and flowed. I could not stop crying. I wiped my nose on the itchy wool-blend sleeve of my coat, but I kept crying. Eventually I picked the bird up, the tiny, little, fragile thing, and placed him on the picnic table. I sat down and stroked the bird and cried and cried.

How could life be so cruel? Why did such a pretty, little, helpless thing have to go and die? As I cried I became angry. How could God, if there was such a thing, let this happen? If God is so nice and kind, how could he let a cute thing just die? Well, I reasoned, maybe he isn't so nice and kind after all. Maybe he is cruel and mean. I had seen boys who would kill things just to watch how it went. They would pull the wings off flies or the legs off daddy longlegs and then watch the insect suffer. I couldn't stand that even though I hated daddy longlegs; they had ruined many a camping trip by crawling on me and making me itchy and frightened of going to sleep. Maybe God was like that; maybe he killed things to watch what happened.

Finally I decided to go inside and blow my nose. I was freezing by the time I stood up and I left the bird on the table. The sky was getting darker or maybe it was going to snow. I went around to the side door of the house and went inside. But I couldn't stop crying and I couldn't leave the bird out there alone. He might be lonely, he might be frightened, something might happen to him. I searched around the house for a box, still in my coat, still with tears on my cheeks. I found a shoe box upstairs in the playroom. It had crayons in it, but I dumped them out (probably on the floor; our playroom was notorious for being a hellhole of messiness) and I took the box back outside in the yard.

I went down the back steps. We had a porch out the kitchen door. It was partially enclosed and very dirty with a musty, old sort of a smell. The stairs to the yard were off to the left and were completely enclosed. So they were dark as well as being dusty and smelly. Once back outside, I carefully, gently placed my tiny dead friend into the box. I put some winter-dead grass in there too, and a few twigs and dried leaves as well. I wanted him to feel that he was at home, with nature around him, even if he was dead. I went back up the stairs to the kitchen and I left the bird on the back porch. I did not think that my parents would like it if I brought it inside. And anyway, the dog might get him.

Later that evening, when my parents got home, they stared at me with disbelief as I told them about what I had found in the backyard. I was crying once again. They could not, for the life of them, understand why I was so upset. They started out puzzled and kind, but after a while the niceness faded into frustration and finally anger at not being able to calm me down. My father asked me what else happened that day. When I told him nothing had happened, it had been a fine day at school, he didn't believe me and said, "Well, something must have happened to get you this upset." And I answered, "Something *did* happen. The bird!" And the tears came again.

My mother was calm in the face of such emotion, but she became upset when I admitted to touching the bird and picking him up. "Did you touch your face, or put your fingers in your mouth after you touched the dead bird?" she asked with alarm in her voice.

I admitted that I had touched my face and may have even put my fingers near my mouth. In fact I was sure that I had touched my mouth after I touched the bird. "Oh, Nica!" she said. "Who knows what diseases that bird could have had? It had to die from something. Did you wash your hands? Go wash them right now!"

I had not washed my hands. So I went to the bathroom. I looked in the mirror. My face was streaked with fresh tears, my eyes were puffy, and my nose was red and running. My too-long hair looked stringy and needed to be brushed. I washed my hands, thinking about the diseases the bird might have had. He hadn't seemed smashed or hurt, so he must have been sick. And now, I thought, I might get sick too. Then will I die as the bird did? I stared at myself hard. No, I would not die. Mom and Dad were just trying to scare me. But still, I remembered sitting at the picnic table, stroking the bird with my fingers and then putting my fingers on my face, across my mouth, even biting a nail as I so often did.

I stopped crying, dried my hands, and calmed down after that. My parents, still somewhat confused at my reaction, agreed to allow me to bury the bird in the backyard the next day. I had a little funeral for it, with Gina and the Allen girls from across the street in attendance. The earth was thawed enough to dig a little hole to put the box in. We were solemn and serious about giving the bird a proper rite of passage to the next realm, but the deep sadness seemed to have left me by then.

Death had been near to me before this, although I had never really seen it, so I had never been really upset. I had not cried when my Grandfather Lalli died six months earlier. He had been kind to us and always had gum for us in his pocket. We would walk around the block in the Bronx on our yearly visits so he could show us off to his neighbors. I did not cry when my Grandpa Lee (my mother's father) died, either. He was a fat, happy man, and we loved his visits. He told us stories and he could make all kinds of animal sounds. His best was a cat. He would meow at any dog he saw on the street or locked in a car, and the dog would bark and bark because Grandpa's cat sound was so real. We also loved that he always brought presents. He had given me a coloring book with a little set of crayons, and Gina got a stuffed animal on what ended up being his final visit. On the way home from driving him to the airport, Gina dropped the stuffed animal out the car window. She howled and cried, but you can't stop on the Kennedy Expressway and pick up a stuffed bear. So she had nothing. And she cried when he died, because she had nothing. I did not cry, because I still had the coloring book and none of the crayons had broken.

I guess the dead bird was the first time I was faced with death. It was the first time I really saw something dead, saw the finality of it, felt the coldness and loneliness of it, and sensed the beauty and sadness of it. I thought about that bird often. When my fish died, when my friend's dog got hit by a car, when one of my neighbor's puppies was stillborn, I did not cry. The tears would not come, but I would think of the precious, small bird in the little box with the grass and the twigs and I would remember the sadness of that afternoon.

chapter 7

bargains with god

During my preteen years, I thought that if you made promises to God to believe in him, he would do you favors. I got the idea from the book *Are You There God? It's Me, Margaret*, by Judy Blume. I read that book in fifth grade, fascinated by the whole idea of growing up (and the bras, periods, and boyfriends) and by the fact that Margaret talks to God and makes deals with him. I decided to try it, too. It would be a simple business transaction. He would get another "believer," and I would get to have whatever it was I wanted. Otherwise, why believe in him at all? He could be like a year-round Santa except that he brought favors and did little deeds that needed to be done.

Whenever my parents went away on trips, I would bargain with God to get them back. On the night they were to return, I would stand in the front bay window, peering out at the street below and waiting for the car or taxi to arrive. I would play a betting game while I watched: "I bet God will make the third car be theirs." And when it was not, I would re-bet: "The sixth car will definitely be theirs." Or I would vary it: "The next car will be blue, then red, then our brown car will come down the street and God will get them home!" I also used this method to get favors with matters of the heart. Even in fourth grade I would "pray" that God would help me by making Neville or Ted or Evan "like" me. And of course I always tried it with schoolwork: "I promise to believe in you if you just help me finish my report on Afghanistan tonight, let me get a good grade, and just plain make me smarter."

I had a friend in fourth and fifth grade named Mona. Mona Tobey was the daughter of two New York Jews who had moved to Chicago and had become intensely right-wing. All the other transplanted New York Jews I knew—friends of my parents, mostly—were left-leaning, even radical, but not these folks. In sixth grade, I clearly remember Mr. and Mrs. Tobey teaching Mona, her older sister, and me about the evils of Communism. In a nutshell, they explained, everyone in a Communist country has to be equal. Therefore if one person has a dog—maybe a Standard Poodle, apricot-colored and adored by the family—that dog would be killed by the evil Commies because that family had something other families did not. So in short, they said, the Commies would come to the United States and kill my dog, Laffy. This was a good occasion for a bargain with God. "God, if you keep the Commies away from my dog, I will believe in you forever!"

Mr. and Mrs. Tobey were certain that the Communists would one day take over the United States. It was not a question of *if*, it was only a question of *when*. I spent many days after school at Mona's house, listening to the paranoid ranting of her parents and watching *The Monkees* reruns on afternoon TV. Mona and I loved *The Monkees*. We loved watching the TV show and had a few of their records. Mona loved Micky Dolenz, while her sister favored Peter Tork, and I liked Mike Nesmith. None of us much cared for Davy Jones. However, when I was playing with my neighbor Linda (on the days we did speak to each other), she would take Davy as *her* Monkee. What we mostly did was listen to each word of each song and try to determine who was singing, who was humming, and who was woo-wooing. Then we pored over the record jackets, occasionally even kissing the photos of those madcap, rag-top fellows.

I had already been through one musical crush with my friend Michelle. We had liked the Osmond Brothers. She had one or two records of the more popular songs, which we must have worn out. Either that or her mother must have smashed them to bits after having been subjected to one too many afternoons of "Puppy Love" and "One Bad Apple" played over and over again. Michelle and I eventually moved on to Elton John and Barry Manilow, but when I was at Mona's house, I could not even mention any other band. It was the Monkees or I was to be thrown to the rapidly approaching Communists.

As much as we loved our respective Monkees, we were also aware that there were real boys near us. Michelle, it was widely reported, had played "Seven Minutes in Heaven" with her neighbor Ethan in his garage. That meant they had kissed and that she had touched the zipper on his pants. Michelle and I had also practiced kissing, using her mother's sofa pillows as stand-ins for boys. One morning after I slept over in Michelle's living room, her mother was particularly irate at the soggy condition of the sofa pillows due to the amount of drooling we had done on them during our practice sessions in the middle of the night.

Meanwhile, Mona mooned over a new boy at school named Harry. Every day at lunch for a year, I would have to listen to her explain in great detail why he was the most perfect boy on the planet. She was still true to Micky Dolenz, she claimed, but Harry was a close second for her affections. I had lists of boys I liked, ranked in order of level of crush. These levels changed frequently. One day Ken would top the list, then he would bring his pet rat to school and be demoted to the bottom. Then Sean would top the list until he said something mean to me and down he would go, and so on.

One day, a warm day in spring, I was standing next to Mona, listening to her extol Harry's every virtue when it hit me. After months of hearing how perfect he was, I had become convinced. And I had decided that he was perfect, but not for Mona. No, he was perfect for me. My eyes became glazed over, and I no longer heard Mona's cracking voice. I stared at Harry, and, as if on TV, the rest of the world dropped into a fuzzy, hazy focus. But it was months before I could tell Mona my true feelings. I was terrified. This was a girl who was sick in her devotion to her beloved. She used to share with me her secret fantasies about Micky Dolenz. And they were disturbing. She used to wish she could find Micky dying, covered in his own blood, and in great pain. He would be lying in the gutter, moaning and crying in the throes of death. She would wrap him in a blanket, usually a ragged one she had found in the street nearby, and take him home to nurse him back to health. Then, of course, he would love her forever and they would never be apart. Not even for a second. Not even for a run to the store to get a bag of Fritos. She would kill me if she found out that I was honing in on *her* Harry.

There were many bargains proposed to God about Harry.

First, of course, was the bargain that would make him like me. Then there were the follow-up bargains that would keep Mona from killing me, and ones that would make us remain friends in the face of Harry and me being together (whatever that meant in sixth grade).

I remember the day I finally told her. We were in front of her house, on our way to school after having had lunch together in her kitchen. She lived in a yellow frame house right around the corner from our school. Her mother didn't work, so she would often make us lunch. I got all my courage up and just blurted it out, "I have a crush on Harry, too!" I tried to make it like we were on the same crush team, but it didn't really work. She was furious with me. I had betrayed her. She wouldn't talk to me. God had let me down.

Our friendship was strained after that. She hooked back up with her old friend Leslie. Leslie was a Nazi. It sounds strange that an elementary school child would have the capacity to be a Nazi, but this young girl had all the zeal and conviction needed to make a perfect Hitler Youth . . . except for the fact that she was half-Japanese. Her mother was Japanese and her father was German, which was part of the reason she felt a kinship with the Nazis. I was never convinced that her father was a sympathizer; Leslie may have simply latched onto her Nazi philosophy as a point of ethnic pride. She used to call me a Commie-Polack-Wop-Jew. This was because Mona had told her I was part Russian Jew, part Polish Jew, and part Italian. Somehow, the fact that Mona, too, was Jewish did not bother Leslie. Perhaps it was the hatred of Communists that freed her from racial slurs. I never quite understood it, but they had decided I was undesirable and they had it in for me.

The worst thing Mona and Leslie did to me after the Harry incident was that they smashed my Abigail Adams figurine. The figurine was made for art class. Mrs. Braun was the art and music teacher and she was a witch. She had blue hair and wore orange lipstick that went all around her mouth, even on the corners. She was one of those ladies who opened her mouth wide to apply the lipstick in a complete circle. She screamed at us every day. She didn't have a creative or expressive bone in her body. Art and music classes with her were less fun than math.

Mrs. Braun had art projects that were the same year after year. Every fall the students created a fall scene in tempera paints; at Christmas we did a winter scene, and later in the year there was the spring scene. After these were handed in, Mrs. Braun had the "best" students take black paint and outline everything in the painting. It looked better, she told us, and made it all clearer. Aside from all the seasonal paintings, we did one sculpture each year. These were papier-mâché figures or, once in eighth grade, pigs made with balloons and egg cartons.

It was 1976 when I was in sixth grade and America was in the middle of the Bicentennial Celebration. Our school was going all out. We made a book of our poetry and writings about our great country. We made a time capsule to bury until the next centennial. We were all taken to see the hit movie *1776*, a musical based on the historic events that shaped our country. We had a school-wide celebration that was like a day off, with a parade around the school yard and a party in the gym. And in Mrs. Braun's class we made figures from our nation's history. I chose Abigail Adams as my historical figure because she was so pretty in the movie. She

had such nice dresses and she got to sing a beautiful song
before she mailed the letter that helped us win the war. So I
made Mrs. Adams. I used wire to make the figure, then
wrapped that with paper towels and newspaper to fill out the
form, then taped it up with masking tape before beginning to
apply the layers of newspaper dipped in a flour and water
paste. My poor Mrs. Adams looked a bit anemic; she was
very thin and sticklike. Her skirt looked more wrinkled than
pleated, and her hair had not quite kept the shape I had
wanted it to have, since I could not get the paper to make the
ringlets that the beautiful actress had in the movie. But she
was carrying the letter. I had made it carefully, written on it
in tiny letters, and glued it to her hand. All in all I was
extremely proud of my creation. I had even made some more
bargains with God to allow my figure to win a ribbon in the
annual art show.

To make sure I did not forget to bring Abigail to school
on the day she was due for the art show, I brought her in a
week early and put her in my locker. It was there, in front
of my locker, that she was nearly destroyed and with her my
hopes for a ribbon at the art show. Leslie took her out of my
locker as I was getting my coat for the end of the day. She
told me that there was no way I would win. She called me
a Pinko-Commie-Jew. Then she held Abigail by the head
and rang her like a bell, loosening her feet from the wooden
block stand. Finally she threw her down, cracking her skirt.
Then Leslie walked away, laughing. I was heartbroken. I
ran home and tried to fix Abigail so I could still put her in
the show. I repainted her skirt and taped her back onto her
stand, but she was a bit crooked and the colors didn't quite
match. I did not win a prize for her. When I had to clean out

my locker at the end of the school year, I threw Abigail Adams away.

I continued making bargains with God through the years. One recurring plea was "Please, God, let me not be flat-chested." Especially after Charlie Pike and some other boys in my homeroom asked me if I had tripped on my way to school, causing whatever breasts I may have had to have been smashed back into my body. That, they said, must be the reason why I was so flat-chested. Mr. Mica was the science teacher and our homeroom teacher. When I told him that the boys had called me flat-chested, he looked at me with his small eyes, and his doughy face broke into a small smile. As he swept his hand across his comb-over, I smelled his aftershave, and he said, simply, "Well, you are." Then he smiled broadly and winked at the boys in a conspiratorial way. I was mortified, to say the least, and I cried in the girls' bathroom but wouldn't say why. Later that night, at home, after tears and prodding from my parents about why I was crying, I told them. And remarkably, my father looked at me sitting on the living room rug in tears and said, "The boys called you flat? Well, you are!" My mother came from the kitchen and yelled at him for being so mean. Then they were fighting, so I got up and went to my room. I hated to be the cause of a fight. It would be easier, I reasoned, if God interceded and caused me to have some growth in the breast department. Then I could be normal, buy a bra, and not hunch over to hide what was missing. Later my mother came to my room and told me, "Don't worry, someday you'll be bigger than all the other girls!" And she stuck her chest out, so I could see what I had coming to me.

God never seemed to be holding up his end of the bargains. Somehow, despite my promises and pledges, I was still without a boyfriend, without good grades, I had no ribbon from the art show, and my body was still that of a too-skinny child. My parents still fought and although they did arrive home safely from every trip, they always seemed to be late, which caused me stress and worry.

I continued to make bargains with God, even after I realized that he was of no help. If I really wanted anything, I would have to work hard and get it myself. But God was like a safety net. I was afraid not to ask for help, fearing that then I really would be screwed. He might become angry and actually go out of his way to prevent whatever I had asked for from happening. "Okay," I would say in my head as I lay in bed unable to sleep. "Okay, if you just do this or that, just this once, then I really will believe in you, really. I'll even go to church. I'll really know that there is something there, see, and then I'll know that I can rely on you."

chapter 8

star wars summer

One night my parents cooked our favorite meal. Even though it was still too cold to grill outdoors, we had spareribs and corn on the cob—in March—and they were being nice to us! They let us have chocolate milk with dinner and asked if we wanted more corn before we had eaten all our meat. Something was definitely up. But, frankly, I was enjoying myself too much to care.

Things had not been going so well for me now that I was in seventh grade. Harry still seemed to be disinterested in my existence, my grades were still only average (as hard as I tried to be less of a procrastinator, I still seemed to leave everything for the night before it was due), Mona was no longer my friend, and my parents hated my new pal, a girl named Barbara.

Barb was "white trash" according to them. Her family was from Tennessee, so they all had strong southern accents. Her father drove a custom RV with swiveling bucket seats and a fancy bed in the back. Her brother lived in the basement and had a full bar down there. Barbara used to sample the different libations, but I thought all the liquors smelled like cough medicine, so I wouldn't taste them. Her parents both worked, and that meant her house was empty after school, except for her old grandmother who lived upstairs and baked coconut cakes. We never saw the grandmother unless we wanted some of that cake, then we'd go on upstairs, get the cake, and come right back down. My parents were also at work, but my mother had hired Jesse, our old cleaning lady, to be there after school to supervise. Jesse was too busy cleaning or cooking to really pay us much attention, but she kept us out of trouble and made us eat the healthy snacks my mother left for us. I preferred Barbara's house with the junk food, the cake, and no Jesse.

So, just as we were finishing our fabulous meal, my dad sat up kind of straight and said that he had something important to tell us. I should have known! Fear ripped through me as I braced myself, suddenly aware that they were bribing us with this nice dinner. They were getting a divorce! Obviously; why else would Dad look so serious? And Mom looked concerned, like she was waiting for Dad to talk so she could burst into tears. Of course, how could I be so stupid? The big announcement was coming, and I still had a mouthful of corn!

"Well," Dad said leaning back. "How would you like to move to New York?"

Gina immediately burst into tears. "I don't want to leave!" she wailed.

I was so relieved that my parents were not getting a divorce that I smiled broadly and nodded my head vigorously. I instantly realized that moving was going to get me out from under all the problems I had at Lincoln School. It would make me different, even special. People would miss me and be sorry they had been mean to me. And I would be in New York City! Mona and I had always dreamed of being New York School Girls just like in the movie *The World of Henry Orient*, which we had seen on TV. After watching it, we dressed up like the two young girls in the movie, wearing blue pleated skirts, white shirts, kneesocks, and dress shoes. Now I would be a real New York School Girl and wouldn't Mona be jealous!

My sister continued to cry and wail, since she did not want to leave her friends, not even for New York. My parents dealt with her for most of the rest of the dinner, so while I ate my corn and ribs, I had time to steep in my thoughts of popularity, revenge, and a new life with a new identity. I was ready to pack and go. Maybe I had even bargained for this one night as I fell asleep; maybe this was the proof I was seeking. But, no, I had not asked for such an escape hatch. It was only now that the possibility had been presented to me that I realized how perfect it was. "Nica is moving!" would be on everyone's lips. "She gets to move to New York! How exotic! How exciting!"

I was brought back to the reality of the dinner table, with my sister sniffing and trying not to start up again, and my father continuing with the announcement. It turned out that they were not really asking us but rather telling us, as Dad had accepted his new job and would be giving notice at his Chicago firm in a few months. The news of the move, therefore, was a family secret. We could tell no one. Since many of our friends were the children of architects, it would surely get back to Dad's electrical engineering bosses that he was planning to leave, and this was not to happen. For months we could not tell our friends, not even our best friends, about the move.

I was dying to spill the beans. If I had fights with friends during that time, I would silently think, "I don't care about you. I am moving far, far away!" I wanted nothing more than to tell my former pal, Mona, that I was leaving—for good! And wouldn't she be sorry! Because only my *real* friends were going to be allowed to come and visit me, and didn't everyone want to go to New York?

Finally, we were allowed to tell. I told Linda first because I felt bad about keeping a secret from her. Through it all (and despite our constant spats) she was my best friend, and a few weeks before, when I was still sworn to secrecy, she had confessed to me that her father was an alcoholic. She told me that she would go out to the garbage each morning to hide the beer cans from the night before, so that when Gina and I came to get her and her sister to walk to school, we wouldn't see all the empties. I had told her then that I had a secret to tell, too, but that I couldn't tell just yet. She had been upset, so I had promised to tell her first. Gina and I told Linda and Lizzie together. And then we all cried. Telling people made it so real. After months of holding the news as a fantasy, the reality of saying, "I am moving away" was hard and sad.

It was May by the time I was telling people. School was almost out, and I would be moving in July. But that spring has three great memories. The first was when Mary Beth and I left school after lunch and went to the Cubs' opening day game. We took the bus to Wrigley Field and bought cheap seats. Then we snuck down into good seats, just above the box seats, and sat there until we were chased away. We ended up sitting on a metal railing above the box seats, and no one seemed to notice us because we stayed there until the game ended. I remember the sun and the green grass and all the people and the two of us, just sitting on that fence and cheering, yelling, and loving every minute of the game.

The second memory was my farewell party. Stephanie threw it at her house. Even though she had switched schools and now went to private school, she was still my friend. It was a surprise party, but I had a pretty good idea that it was going to happen, because my mother cannot keep a secret to save her life. I thought that Stephanie and I were going to a play at her school that night, but every time Friday's plans were mentioned, my mother would giggle and grin. So I was hardly surprised to see all my friends sitting in Stephanie's rec room. We ate hot dogs and drank soda and then we played records and danced until it was time to go home. I got to dance with Harry to one of the popular ABBA songs. I was completely happy.

The third memory I have is of seeing *Star Wars* with my father. *Star Wars* came out that spring, and I first heard about it from Ted. He tried to describe the light sabers, but couldn't. They had to be seen, he said, to be believed. The whole movie, he added, was awesome and unlike anything we would have ever seen before.

Dad and I went to see it one weekend day. We walked a long way to the movie theater. It was far outside our neighborhood. We had lunch at Wendy's. I had never been to a Wendy's before, and it quickly became my favorite fast food. I remember the square hamburgers and the ultra-thick shakes. I liked it better than McDonald's because you could order your burger plain (that is, with ketchup only). After we ate, we saw the movie. I sat in the dark, and as the music began, a huge, incredibly huge spaceship seemed to actually fly over our heads. It was unreal. Even when I watch *Star Wars* on TV on a tiny screen, I remember that feeling in the theater that first time I saw it. I loved every second of the movie. Luke Skywalker was so cute, and Princess Leia was so gorgeous. My favorites were Chewbacca and Han Solo, those wisecracking, troublemaking rebels.

Gina saw it soon after I did, and we became obsessed. We had the *Star Wars* record album, *Star Wars* trading cards, *Star Wars* cups and T-shirts and posters. Every extra penny we had that summer went to Lucasfilm to pay for another viewing of the movie or a product with a tie-in.

We brought our *Star Wars* obsession with us when we left Chicago. We left in July, after we had spent three weeks at summer camp. We returned from camp to find our entire house packed and ready for the movers. There was a yard sale, the movers arrived, and then we were in my empty room crying with our neighbors, Linda and Lizzie, before we got in the car and started to drive to the East Coast.

My parents had bought a house in Greenwich Village. We had been out to New York to see it in May, but they would not actually own the house until late August. Dad was living at a friend's apartment during the week and had been commuting back to Chicago for most weekends while he started his new job. We left our house at the end of July and stayed for the rest of the summer with my mother's sister, Aunt Leila, in Portland, Maine. She owned a big house right near the ocean, and we were going to live there with her and whichever of my four older cousins were around that summer.

Mom, Gina, the dog, and I piled in the car and started the drive to Maine. We had done the drive numerous times before and we always stopped at Niagara Falls for the night and then finished the drive the next day. The one who was most upset by the move was the dog. Each time we stopped the car, he would bound out and run as if we were home and the house were right there, then he would stop and look around and sit dejectedly. By the time we got to Niagara Falls and checked into the cheap motel, Laffy was despondent. He wouldn't eat and he hated getting out of the car. I was happy to be at a motel with a pool, and we got to eat at Ponderosa, which I liked because everything was served plain: no onions, no green things. The next day we got to my aunt's house late at night and had to pull the dog out of the car. He finally settled down and ate, but whenever he got back in the car, it was a real trick to get him out.

The rest of the summer was spent at the beach or going to the mall to see *Star Wars* or to buy any new *Star Wars* goodies we could find. I think by the time we got to New York City in late August, we had seen the movie five or six times. We could recite entire scenes and often did. We each had a favorite part: mine was when the heroes are stuck in the trash dump, Gina's was when they are in the bar with all the strange creatures. And we had favorite lines, many of them belonging to the dashing Han Solo, but we also repeated some of Leia's snappy comebacks dozens of times a day. My strongest memories of that summer are sitting at the top of the stairs outside our bedrooms on the second floor of the large and somewhat dingy house in Maine. The strong summer sunlight would stream in, and we would listen to the *Star Wars* record I had received for my birthday over and over again. We knew what was happening in the movie at each strain or swoop in the music. It was blissful.

The best thing about *Star Wars* was how simple it made

life seem. There were the good guys fighting and struggling against the bad guys. And even though they were less armed, less powerful, and had older, smaller jets, the good guys could still win. Because if you were good—truly good—then you could always win. Evil could be conquered by goodness. Look at Darth Vader, he got left spinning into deep space, never to be heard from again! Our cousins quickly pointed out that Darth Vader would most certainly be back in the next film. We could hardly believe our luck—there would be a next film!! And we were quite sure that good would win over evil once again.

The *Star Wars* record album became a portable shrine for Gina and me. We traveled a lot that summer, heading back and forth between Maine, New Hampshire, and Connecticut (where we had other relatives to visit), and finally to New York City. It didn't matter where we were; we were not "home"; we did not even really have a home, so our *Star Wars* record album became sacred. The cover even had scenes from the movie so we could relive them when we were not near the mall and its movie theater.

I was now thirteen, having had my birthday in the middle of our extended move to New York, and I was getting scared of what lay ahead. I would be the new girl at a new school. I would get my new start as I had wanted, but I realized I would be different, and it began to dawn on me that I might be different in a not-so-good way. I was so tall, so skinny, and still flat as a board. I wore clothes that my mother thought were cute but that were fairly nerdy according to my older cousin Pam. She wore straight-legged jeans and makeup and was forever trying to instruct me on how to dress cool. But I was a hopeless case. I liked my flared pants with the two zippers, one on each hip. I liked wearing a T-shirt over a long-sleeved shirt. I liked my red overalls with the white stitching that Mom had bought me at Marshall Field's. They looked good even if they did accentuate my lack of bust.

We arrived in New York on a steamy dog-day in August. Our furniture had arrived and was in the correct rooms, but little had been unpacked. Gina and I were to live on the top floor, which was the hottest in the summer and the coldest in the winter. We each had our own large rooms; mine was in the front of the house and Gina's overlooked the garden. I remember my first night in that room as one filled with terror. I was sure that there were large bugs—cockroaches—waiting to climb up the posts of my bed and crawl all over me. I could not sleep. It was so hot and noisy. Why had I chosen the room facing the street? And I was waiting, waiting for that creepy feeling of a bug in a bed.

The first thing we did after we helped unpack was to drive over to my new school. We had walked to Gina's. She was going into fifth grade and would be at Public School 41, around the corner from our new house. It was not a little red schoolhouse, like Lincoln School had been, but a more modern bluish building that looked friendly and inviting. We drove to my school because it was farther away. It was also in a creepy neighborhood, and my mom probably felt safer looking at it through the car window. Intermediary School 70 looked like a prison. It was a drab, grayish-yellow color with huge black gates across the front of it. It looked neither friendly nor inviting. I was terrified.

Mom wanted us each to know a few kids at our new schools, so she called an old friend with daughters who were the same ages and went to the schools we would be attending. We met them one day at their country house in Connecticut. Abby, the younger girl, seemed nice, and she and Gina played together. Stacey, who was my age, was a mean-spirited, frightening girl. She told me every terrifying story she could drum out of her memory (or her fantasy world) about the horrid things that would happen to me at my new school.

"The Puerto Rican girls will make you smoke," she warned me. "And if you don't, they will beat you up." There was more. "Milk will be poured down your backpack as you walk around from class to class, so get a lock." "Don't wear any jewelry to school, it'll get stolen." "If you ever eat in the lunch room, watch out for flying food. All my friends eat with a teacher in a classroom." And, "Learn to walk with your arms crossed over your chest, that way you won't get molested between classes." After a few hours of these stories, I was ready to move back to Chicago. I missed my tiny, friendly school. Even the mean kids back in Chicago sounded nice compared to this New York crowd.

One day, right before school started, we went to the public swimming pool near our house with our friends Nancy and Jane. Nancy and Jane had lived in Chicago and had moved to New York a few years before we had. Our parents were good friends, and we had visited one another many times. Their parents were now divorced, and the girls lived with their mom in a loft on Spring Street. They had a hammock and a jukebox in the loft. I had never even heard the word *loft* before, but after seeing theirs, I wanted to live in one. Nancy and Jane, who went to private schools, were eager to do something fun with us before we all had to go back to school. So off we went to swim on one of the last days of summer.

We got to the pool and went to the locker room to change. The locker room was dark and a little dirty, but we didn't see any of the much-dreaded cockroaches. We changed fast and tried not to look too closely in the corners, just in case any were lurking. We went out to the pool and sat by the edge. The water was very cold despite the heat, and so we were easing ourselves into the coolness. Out of nowhere, a girl swam up to us, right up to where we were sitting, and she dug her long fingernails into Nancy's thigh. Nancy yelped and tears appeared in her eyes. None of us knew what to do. Nancy was the oldest among us—she had been put in charge by our mothers—and now she was wounded and the mean girl was coming back.

"Let's go!" Nancy ordered us back to the dressing room once she could speak. "We don't want any more trouble."

We followed Nancy back to our lockers. We were scared and silent. When we got there, we stood motionless, trying to decide what to do; should we really leave, should we tell someone about the attack, or should we just go back to the pool and try again? But the mean girl had followed us. She came right up to us in the locker room and swore at us, taunted us, and threatened us. She said, with what I later came to recognize as a Puerto Rican accent, that she would beat us up—kick our white asses—and that we had better be careful. She wouldn't even let us open our lockers. Gina, Jane, and I were scared enough to cry.

Then, all of a sudden, Nancy snapped. She went from trembling and holding the still-red scratches on her thigh to yelling back at the girl.

"Listen!" she yelled at the mean girl. "Stop this right now, we did not do anything to you, you know. We don't even know why you are bothering us. Why don't you go away and let us be? And another thing," Nancy was really on a roll, "these girls just moved here. Just moved here last week, and this is the impression that you are giving them of our city, of the kind of people here in New York. You ought to be ashamed, really. It is not right!"

Amazingly, the girl did not slug Nancy. She did not swear or taunt us again. She actually apologized to us. She felt bad, she said, and she was sorry. She even told us we could come back to the pool, that she would not bother us again. It was just like *Star Wars*, when the battle of good against evil was won by the nice, the sweet, and the kind-hearted. We did go back to the pool, and she was good to her word. She waved to us from across the cement deck and kept an eye on us; she did not want any *other* mean kids bothering her new friends.

chapter 9

bible ski trip

I made it through eighth grade and had some friends by the time spring came around. The first months of school were a little lonely, since I was the new girl and had to hang out with the other oddballs. I was odd because of my clothes and the broad *A* of my Chicago accent, not because I was from a family of nothing. Religion was never a topic of discussion, except when it was the main theme of the book we had to read for English class. That year we read *Stranger in a Strange Land*, a science fiction book about a messiahlike spaceman who comes back to Earth. I hated the book and thought it was just plain weird. When the spaceman tries to understand religion, he uses the term *grok* to explain the concept of an all-knowing, all-seeing God. My classmates thought that was cool, so everybody had little pins saying, "I grok" on them. I had a pin, and since it was given to me by one of the popular girls, of course I took it, but I never wore it. I didn't "grok" and was glad when we read *Wuthering Heights* as our next book.

I was pretty comfortable with my family being nothing by the time I was in my teens. None of my friends went to church or to any religious service by the time we were in high school. The only people in high school who were religious at all were the black kids, who sang in the Gospel Choir and carried their Bibles with their schoolbooks, and some of the Spanish-speaking kids, who wore big crosses around their necks. Our school was incredibly mixed—black, white, Hispanic, Asian—but each group mostly stayed with its own kind.

I did not think about religion very much during my high school years, since I was too busy worrying about how Ronald Reagan had become our president, about gun control, and when the next "No Nukes" rally would be. These were the important issues to me and my friends. Or, of course, which boy we had a crush on, what new shoes we wanted, or when we could see the latest *Star Wars* or *Raiders of the Lost Ark* movie. I was in the tenth grade when Ronald Reagan won the presidential election and moved into the White House. That was a big eye-opener for us. We went to the High School of Music and Art, the *Fame* school. We were artists, liberals, and counterculture. We thought we were the norm, we thought everyone else in America was like us. We did not yet realize that New York is in a bubble; it is not part of mainstream America. No one we knew—no teachers, none of our friends' parents, none of our parents' friends—had voted for Reagan. We were baffled. How, then, did this guy get to be president? Who voted for him?

Our classmates were either punk, new wave, hippie, or disco. We were all defined by what music we listened to and what clothes we wore. My friends and I were the "normal" kids, a small, nerdy group who listened to Linda Ronstadt, Billy Joel, and Fleetwood Mac before we got a little "cool" and bought albums by Blondie, The Cars, and The Police. We dressed "normal" too—in jeans and sweatshirts. In tenth grade, I read *The Preppy Handbook* from cover to cover. My sister had gotten it from a friend and, presto, overnight I became a "prep." The preppy style was completely unknown in my high school; I was the only person there wearing Izod shirts, argyle sweaters, loafers, and headbands. It was a way of being different without dying my hair bright pink and it had the added benefit of driving my parents crazy. They hated my button-down look. They wanted me to dress "funky" or "cool." One night, when I was on my way out to the downtown club CBGB to see some high school bands play, my parents called me into the study where they were watching TV. I was wearing my favorite striped rugby shirt and a pair of jeans. I had put on a little eyeliner and I was wearing hanging earrings, so I considered myself dressed up.

"You are wearing *that*?" my mother asked.

I looked down at my clothes and nodded. I thought I looked good.

"God, Nica," she said, "you look so boring! Why don't you wear something more, I don't know, funky, pretty, or something. You can't go out like that! Why don't you borrow one of my silk blouses at least."

I shrugged and went out. Most people's moms would be glad that they had daughters who dressed so conservatively. I had the mom who would be happier if I dressed like a slut, I thought, as I met up with Deborah. (She had style, according to my mom, and why couldn't I dress more like her?) CBGB was so dark and crowded and loud and smelly that it didn't matter what I was wearing.

My sister had a good friend named Antonia Bianchi. Antonia was Italian, but both her parents really were from

Italy—not like our dad who was born here. She had an older brother who went to a private school uptown. Her brother, Carlo, was *very* preppy. He and his friends were also very cute, so I used to get reports on him and the other preppy guys he knew from Gina; what they wore, where they went out, anything that I could use to be more preppy.

One year Antonia invited Gina to come along on a ski trip during the Christmas holidays. The trip was run by Carlo's church and it was cheap. So Mom sent Gina along. Gina and Antonia came back with great enthusiasm. They had loved every minute of it, the skiing, the food at the lodge, the singing, and storytelling in the evenings. And the other kids and the counselors were so nice! The next year, Mom sent me, too.

When we arrived in Vermont after many hours in a van, Gina and Antonia and the littler kids were dropped off first. I was with the high school kids. That seemed fine to me, since I didn't much want to spend the week with my sister and her bratty pals. I would be better off on my own. There was one girl I liked, despite the fact that her first name was almost the same as our president's name: Regan. I knew from my studies of *The Preppy Handbook* that this kind of name was common among the preppy set. And I was among the preppy set. I suddenly didn't seem preppy at all. These folks were the real deal: Muffies, Chips, and Bifs, with plaid everything and add-a-bead necklaces to boot. Anyway, since I went to public school, I was not really a "prep."

I settled into the dorm-style room with Regan. She and I took the top and bottom of one bunk and spent the rest of the first evening talking about the *Chronicles of Narnia*. We both loved the books, and I had brought a few along to reread over the break from school.

Dinner was fine, in fact, the food at the lodge was really good. They said grace before we ate, but for many years at summer camp we had sung grace each night, so the short little poem they recited did not seem strange to me. Everyone at the table was extremely nice, in fact, everyone in the whole place seemed very nice. It was strange to be around so many nice, cheerful people. That should have been my first clue that something was wrong.

After dinner we retired into a large sitting room. There were quite a few of us, and so we sat on couches, the floor, or on folding chairs. We sang a few Christmas songs (it *was* just after the holiday) and maybe a Beatles tune. But then they sang a few songs I didn't know that had Christ and God mentioned throughout. That should have been my second clue that something was wrong.

Then there were some "testimonials" by people who had accepted Jesus into their hearts and were now happier, better people for it. People told of their self-loathing, their anger, and their destructive behavior from before they became Christians, and got choked up and misty-eyed when they spoke of their wonderful, peaceful, loving existences since their conversions. Even Carlo spoke. He sat on the arm of a couch and told us about the drugs, the escape from the reality of his sins, and the mean and hateful things he had done before. Then he talked about walking with Jesus and the happiness he had found. He revealed that since he was "born again" he had found a better path. He even cried. I sat frozen in my folding chair in the middle of the crowd of heads nodding and eyes being wiped.

Jesus? Born Again? What the hell? Had I missed something on the ride up here? Had they all been praying and proselytizing for the seven long hours? Maybe they had been speaking in code, but I couldn't recall any clue that would have prepared me for this.

I was confused. Antonia and her family had said this was a church ski trip, but they never mentioned that conversion would be on the agenda. I assumed it was just a nice bunch of kids who wanted to ski and happened to go to the same church. I worried that they were doing this to Gina. Then I worried about the fact that, technically, because my mother was Jewish, I was a Jew by birth. By Jewish law, if your mother is Jewish then you are a Jew. Would they kick me out, send me home? The ride up had been too long to turn around and go back to the city. I wanted to ski. There was tons of snow on the ground and the conditions would be good. What was I going to do?

I hoped that my panic was not showing on my face as my heart raced and I broke into a sweat. Then Bill stood up. He had driven the van up from New York and had been the one in charge. He was definitely in charge now as he instructed us what to do next.

"Everyone who is sure in their relationship with God and his Son, Christ our Lord, stay up here. Anyone who is unsure of their relationship with God and Jesus please go downstairs." Then he headed downstairs.

There was the usual rumble of a crowd dispersing. I continued to sit in the folding chair, trying to process what was happening. I had come along to ski, to hang out, even to sing. But this, what was this? Was it a conversion? Were they out to "make me" Christian? Anyway, I felt sure in my relationship with God and Jesus: sure that I was not interested in having any relationship with either of them.

Somehow I sensed that this answer would not be welcomed. So I stood up and smiled as best I could at Regan, who was staying upstairs with those "sure" people.

There were not many of us in the room downstairs. Besides me, there were a few other nonbelievers along with Bill and Fritz, who had been in the van from New York with us, too. He was jovial, tall, and blond. I had instantly liked him, not only because he was so handsome but because he was so darn nice. He had also promised to help any beginner skiers on the slopes, and I was definitely that. But now he was sitting there trying to convince me . . . of what? That Jesus had died on the cross for my sins and that I should love Jesus and then my sins will be taken by him and I will be cleansed and then I could go to heaven when I die? That was the gist of it, but it took them three nights "downstairs" to get it all out.

Before they started in on us that first night, they asked us what it was we did believe in. This stumped me for the simple reason that no one had really asked me that question before. So I was not particularly articulate as I tried to describe what I thought was my special brand of religious skepticism.

"Well, I kind of believe in God," I said, hoping nobody would hear the "kind of" part and just nod happily. "I mean, I think there is something, someone out there." They nodded solemnly, so I kept going. "As for Jesus, I, um, I don't know . . ." The "I don't know" line had worked for many years: just say, "I don't know" and the conversation ended. However, this time it did not work.

After that, they spent the remainder of the night laying out the many, many pitfalls of life. They outlined the many

ways that one could sin. They clarified the fact that even
thinking a mean or nasty thought was, in God's eyes, a sin.
And sinning was punishable by eternal damnation. I was
angry and frustrated to learn that almost everything I did
was a sin. Even if I just sat there thinking angry thoughts, I
was sinning. I was feeling more and more confused, and less
and less able say anything other than "I don't know . . . ,"
which came out weaker and weaker every time I said it.

The next day we finally got to hit the slopes. The skiing
was fabulous. During the daylight hours, I was happy and
having fun. The meals at the lodge continued to be good,
with home-baked breads, muffins, and cakes plus hearty,
wintry dishes—chicken potpie or beef stew—that really
filled you up and warmed you after a day on the cold ski
slopes. But as soon as the sun went down, as soon as dinner
was over, I would get nervous, sweaty, and even a bit dizzy.
I dreaded the night ahead. No TV, no fun and games, just
Bill and his relentless lectures and sermons.

The second night I was tired, since I had skied all day. I
had dreaded coming downstairs and had taken my time getting there. I claimed to have forgotten something back in the
room and wasted ten minutes trying to "find" it. When I did
settle into my seat and the lecture about hell began, I was
annoyed. I did not want to learn about the eternal fires of
hell, and yet that is what I got to hear about all night. I
learned all about hell, how awful it was going to be, how
despondent, lonely, and miserable sinners were in hell, forever suffering and never being offered a way out. That was
it, it was final. Once you were there, you were, in a word,
damned. I couldn't help but feel a creeping sense of hope-
lessness. I was going to suffer when I died, and there was

nothing I could do to stop it, since I seemed to sin every moment. I didn't want to suffer! As I sat there miserable over my doomed plight, it dawned on me that I didn't actually *believe* in any of what they were saying. Oh, yeah, I said to myself, I don't buy into this whole heaven and hell thing. I may not be sure about the ruler of the universe, but I am sure that when you die you are just dead.

After Bill's lecture, I finally had a chance to speak. I tried to use logic to defend my nonbeliever position. The Bible seemed so illogical to me; even though I had never read the book I did know some of the stories. So I tried to use Jonah and the Whale as an example of how the Bible cannot be literally true.

"It is a parable," I declared. "You can't possibly think that Jonah was literally eaten by a whale."

Fritz, nice, cute Fritz, said he did believe it. If it was in the Bible, it was true. God wrote it, and we were not to question its veracity. "It is the word of God," he said.

"Okay," I muttered, sad that Fritz was one of them. "I get it, the word of God, even if it is totally ridiculous."

"Try to open your heart," Fritz leaned in a little closer to me and smiled. "Don't be so harsh and so closed to the love of Christ."

I smiled back at him. I wished that we were somewhere else, that he wasn't trying to convert me. Maybe he could just have a crush on me instead. He kept smiling, and I knew that he was only being nice to me so that he could get me to see things his way. I wondered if he would get a little prize for saving another soul.

The last night downstairs was spent offering me a way out of all that eternal writhing and pain. All I had to do, it seemed, was take Jesus into my heart. Then I would have a free ticket to eternal salvation. But God, and Jesus too, could tell if I was lying. They would know if I did not truly have Jesus in my heart, and so I had to work at giving my heart over to him completely. It would be hard work, they told me, but look at the reward! Eternal life with Jesus!! Of course, I would have to die to get my payoff, but this life is so short; it is the afterlife that really matters anyway.

I tried to shoot down the arguments they used on me, since I did not want to take Jesus into my heart and become a Christian. But I didn't really have much in the way of ammunition against them, since my logic argument had fallen short. The "sales" pitch they had given me did not make sense, that was for sure. But to articulate why was tricky; I didn't seem to speak the language that they did, and all the doublespeak and old words like *shall* and *begot* just confused me more. I wanted to say, "This is just too dumb-assed for words," but I just couldn't. I wanted to stand up and yell, "Listen you freaks, this is all good and well for you—this eternal life Jesus dying on the cross stuff—but I don't want it. I don't need it! Leave me alone."

But how could I yell at these nice, *nice* folks? They were just trying to help. Just like my old friends, the Jesus Freaks at my door, from way back when I was so small and alone. They were just trying to help, too. The problem was that I couldn't yell because I wasn't sure. I was sure that I didn't want to become a Christian, but I was unsure what I did want to be. I was unclear about what I did believe.

I wound up feeling very frustrated that I had so little understanding of religion. My arguments against them were weak, since I had no religious training at all. Maybe if I had been even a little bit "really" Jewish, maybe then I could have had more to say against them, against what they were trying to get me to accept as my belief. I didn't want to argue anymore, I didn't want to have to justify what or who I was to anyone, much less these strangers. Why was my salvation so important to them, anyway? What I really wanted to do was go to sleep so I could wake up the next day and get to the ski area.

By the end of the third night downstairs, I was in a pretty defensive position. I was slumped over, arms crossed, and head down. I kept shutting my eyes tight as if that would make it stop, like a pinch out of a daydream. There was no point in arguing, since anything I said was shot down anyway. I couldn't make them stop trying to convince me that the Bible was the word of God, that Jesus would save my wretched and sinful soul, and that I would be a happier, better person if I converted to Christianity. Not unless I gave in and agreed to be saved. And that was one thing I was sure would not happen—not ever.

I was really mad. How had they tricked me into this? By offering a cheap ski trip, that's how. I was furious at my mother for signing me up without finding out more about it. Hadn't she bothered to ask Mrs. Bianchi what church was sponsoring the trip? No, of course not, the Bianchis were perfect, anything they did was fabulous, so here I was. I was angry at Carlo Bianchi too, Mr. Cool-Preppy Jerk!! He was supposed to be *Catholic*, like all Italians, not some wacky, reborn Jesus Freak. He had not said more than three words to me the entire week, either. I could not believe how alone I felt.

Finally, it was the last night. I had had my three nights in the basement and now it was New Year's Eve. There would be a party; Bill had said it was going to be fun and special. I couldn't imagine what they meant, but I thought maybe they would let us have a little champagne. I wasn't much of a drinker, but my parents always let me have champagne on New Year's or other special occasions.

After dinner we all gathered in the big room, the upstairs room where we had started out all together. At least I could sit with Regan. She really was nice; she seemed normal, no talk of Christ or hell or fire and brimstone. And at night, who knows, maybe she and the other "sure" ones were watching TV and drinking beers. So here we all were, ready for the last night of 1980. There was more of the singing with the same mix of songs. This time during the Jesus ones, I didn't even try to sing, I just sat there and looked blank. But there was juice and time for chitchat and then some more singing. So it was mostly okay. Then, as it was getting late, they quieted us all down and made an announcement. This was the "special" part of the evening.

They asked us all to come forward and start the year off fresh, cleansed, ready for Jesus. They had some water. They had some towels. They were *baptizing* people! Right there in the sitting room of the ski lodge. The evening collapsed around me. The week collapsed around me. I just wanted to go home. They were all singing, and those who were being baptized were lining up in the front of the room. Everyone seemed so pleased with the evening, like it was such a success, such a great way to start the year. People tried to talk to me, they tried to convince me to be spiritually cleansed, but I was shut down and wouldn't engage. I answered them politely, since I didn't want to fight or offend anyone. I didn't want to dampen their joy or ruin their evening. I had a vague sort of a smile on my face as I refused to go forward. Slowly, slowly, as others moved to the front of the room, I pushed back. Farther and farther back I slid, whenever I felt no one was looking, until my back was against the far wall and I could sit and just stare at my slippers. Mom had given me mukluks for Christmas; she had said they would be perfect for padding around the ski lodge as we played board games or told jokes in front of the fire. Little did she know that I was sitting in a makeshift church resisting the pleas to shun my Jewish heritage and my nonreligious upbringing and to join the Jesus Team.

Finally, it was over. I was allowed to go to bed, and the next day we drove back to the city. The ride home was fine. Bill didn't make any more attempts to convert me, and I was back with Gina and Antonia. They had had a great time, again. They had skied every day and at night they popped popcorn, sang songs, and told jokes. There had been no upstairs/downstairs for them, no proselytizing, no baptism, just skiing and wholesome fun and games.

I was not happy when I arrived home. As I told my parents the whole story, they sat with their mouths hanging open. It was not what they had expected, since Gina had never been put through anything like it. They had no idea, no idea that this nice group of kids would turn out to be a bunch of "Jesus Freaks"! After telling them the story of my last four days, I was exhausted and wanted to go to bed. I would be returning to high school in another day or two, so sleep was of utmost importance until then. My parents were still sitting at the table in the back of the house when I got up to go to my room.

"By the way, you didn't take Communion, did you?" my father asked with a fake worried look on his face.

"No," I said. "They offered that New Year's Eve baptism, but no Communion. Not that I would have taken it."

"Good," my dad said, rubbing his unshaven chin and trying to suppress a laugh. "Because if you had taken the Communion, you would have been struck down dead by God, you know. You were never christened as a child, so you are a heathen. You aren't allowed to partake in the flesh and blood of the Lord Jesus. A lightning bolt would have come and struck you down."

"Okay, Dad," I said, rolling my eyes. "I'll see you in the morning." I was so relieved to be home that Dad's teasing was music to my ears. I was so happy that I had not been made one of them, so happy that the sermons, lectures, and threats of eternal suffering had failed to win me over. It strengthened my resolve to remain nothing, even though I still had some trepidation over the idea of not believing in anything. If the ideas of born-again Christianity were what I had learned over the five days in Vermont, I knew at least that I could rule that one out as a possibility.

chapter 10

real-life death

One thing about being a teenager, which I learned from rereading the journals I kept during those tumultuous years, is that teenagers are very, very self-involved. I cannot believe that in twelfth grade I had a dying grandmother, a dead dog, a boy from my homeroom class murdered not twenty blocks from my school, and a driving teacher killed in a car accident, yet all I managed to scribble in my journal was how much I was "in love" with this boy, or what should I do about calling or not calling him, or what should I wear in case I ran into him. Maybe the real events of my life were just too real for me to write about. The fantasy of a love life was safer because it was so much a design of my own imagination.

When my classmate Steven was beaten to death at the 125th Street subway station, we were all shocked. He couldn't really be dead. He was at school just the week before, even on the very day of the beating he had been in homeroom, smiling, laughing, and playing the piano. Then, wham, he was hospitalized after a Harlem gang chased him all over the subway station, caught him, and beat him up. It had happened on the night that we held our school talent show. Our school was in Harlem, but Steven was from Brooklyn. He and his "posse" had tangled with a rival Harlem "posse" somewhere near the school. Some people said it was at the talent show, others reported words exchanged outside. Having a "posse" did not mean that Steven was in a gang; "posse" was just another word for your group of friends. He told me that one morning in Miss Collin's science class. We were working on a project that day and chatting when he used the word *posse*. I had no idea what he was talking about. He explained, "You know, your posse is like your boys, the guys you hang with, your friends."

Steven didn't die right away. He was in the hospital for a few days. It turns out he was a hemophiliac, a bleeder. And so he bled to death internally due to the injuries from being punched, kicked, and smacked. He probably wouldn't have died if he hadn't been a hemophiliac. I remember the day he died. I was in the girls' bathroom on the second floor when the news spread. The bathroom was usually full of girls smoking and cutting classes, and that day there were the usual characters hiding out in there. As I dried my hands on the rough, brown paper towel, I heard some of the girls in the hallway screaming. Then the girls around me started yelling, "He's dead! He's dead!" And one girl dropped down to the ground in a dead faint. They carried her out in front of me. I stood with all the panic and chaos around me and felt numb. The dean showed up in a few minutes and shooed us all to class. I cannot imagine that any of us heard a thing the teachers said for the rest of the day. Outside of school that afternoon, everyone was in tears.

I did not know Steven well, but we had been together in

homeroom for almost four years, from the first day of ninth grade. When we had homeroom in the tower music room one year, he played the piano every day until the music teacher came up from downstairs and told him to stop. "That piano didn't hurt you, so don't hurt it!" she would say every single day. Then she would leave, and Steven and his friends would go back to playing. They could really play, though. It wasn't as if they were just pounding on the instrument. My favorite was when they played the *Peanuts* song, and they played it almost every day.

We were the *Fame* school, after all. We may not have danced out on the street after school as they did in the movie, but we did have a musical homeroom courtesy of Steven and his friends. He was such a nice kid, and that is what I really remember. He was just a nice kid with a big smile. To this day, I cannot believe he was killed like that, in the same subway station I used every day of those four years. Killed by other black kids who didn't like his address.

The spring Gospel Chorus concert was dedicated to Steven. I went and sat right in front of the stage because there were no more seats. I sat looking up at the darkness and then—pow!—the lights came on and the choir sang loudly, then they swayed in time and clapped. The music was powerful and inspirational. I knew it was all about Jesus and God and I didn't care what they were saying. The experience—the sound, the lights, the memory of my classmate—was very moving. I cried and cried sitting there on that cold stone floor of the Music and Art Auditorium. And I knew that God and Jesus couldn't help poor Steven; they couldn't give him back his future. Nothing could undo what was done.

During senior year, I took driver's education classes. I needed the classes so I could get my license a year early, at age seventeen. If I passed the classes and passed my test, maybe I would be allowed to drive to school. I took the classes at a private school near my house on Tuesdays and Thursdays. Tuesday was classroom instruction. It was as dull as could be and taught by a moronic guy (whose name was actually Guy) who thought he was very funny and witty. His jokes were old and stale, so we doodled and passed notes through the whole two hours. Thursday we had real driving lessons. There were four of us and Ronnie, the other instructor, in the car. We would take turns driving in the East Village, around Tompkins Square Park, with a stop for pastries at Veniero's on East 11th Street. The East Village was not the neighborhood it is today. It wasn't even called the East Village; it was called the Lower East Side. There were drug dealers and lowlifes on every corner. It was a scary part of town. When we changed drivers, we would count to three and then open the doors and run around the car as fast as we could. Then we would jump back in, slam the doors, and lock ourselves safely back inside.

Ronnie was a great instructor. He was patient and calm and never yelled at us. Even when we went through a stop sign or swerved into oncoming traffic, he calmly stopped the car with the brake on his side and pointed out to the driver-in-training that maybe they wouldn't want to do that again. We had a great time on Thursdays. When it was time to take our driving tests, he offered to meet us at the Department of Motor Vehicles course under the Williamsburg Bridge so we could use the same car we had learned in.

The first time I took the test, I went with my mother in

the big, brown family car. I failed the test miserably, since I rolled through a stop sign and failed to signal at a turn. The next time I had the test, I went with Ronnie. It was a day off from school, and I did well—really well. I was sure I had passed that time, even though there was snow on the ground and the parking had been tricky with the piles of snow at the curb. He dropped me off afterward in Little Italy in front of Umberto's Clam House. Ronnie was an Italian from Staten Island, and we were always joking about being Italian. Umberto's had been the scene of a famous mob hit, so as a joke, my parents always crossed the street in front of Umberto's, claiming that they didn't want any stray bullets to get them. So Ronnie and I had a good laugh at that as I got out of the car to walk up to my job. On days off and after school I helped an artist in her studio in SoHo. As I walked there I was so happy. I was sure I had passed the driving test. Ronnie was such a nice teacher, such a great guy.

It was a few weeks later that I found out he was dead. The other girl from the car, Jenny, called me after school one day, in tears. She went to Stuyvesant, which was not far from my house, and she told me she had to come over. I asked what was wrong, but she wouldn't tell me over the phone.

"I'll be there in fifteen minutes," she said.

I looked out my window until she got there. I could not imagine what she had to tell me in person. I thought she had broken up with her boyfriend or something like that. But when I saw her, I knew it was not an affair of the teenaged heart. She looked destroyed, so sad and droopy and deflated. I ran to the front door and she stumbled inside. She threw her coat on the rack and hugged me.

"What on earth is going on?" I asked.

"It's Ronnie," she said with fresh tears. "He is dead."

I had to sit down. It was too awful. I felt like I'd been punched in the stomach for the second time that year. We cried and cried that afternoon. We didn't know what else to do. We wanted to send flowers to his family. We wanted them to know how much we had loved our driving classes, how Ronnie had made it fun, how he made us feel special and competent, how he always had confidence in us, unlike other adults in our lives.

We never did send flowers. And as spring came, there was another death looming that overtook Ronnie's. My grandmother, my mom's mom, had been living with cancer for over twenty years. She had breast cancer and had a mastectomy when she was about fifty. Now she was in her seventies and the cancer had returned. And after fighting all the fight she could fight, she was dying.

My grandmother—we called her Nan—was one of my favorite people in the world. She was like another best friend to me. I slept over at her house two or three times a month, so we could go to the movies, plays, and the ballet together. We shopped together and met for lunch. She listened to me and shared my interests and my worries.

Nan was a very refined lady. She had her hair done every week at the St. Moritz Hotel. She liked fine china and dark wood antiques. She had velvet couches and long manicured nails. She hated messes, chaos, and ugliness. To me she was first-class; whatever she liked was special and elegant in my eyes.

When I was young, she lived in Elmhurst, Queens. But she longed to move into Manhattan. At about the same time we arrived in New York from Chicago, she moved to 66th Street and West End Avenue. She lived right behind Lincoln Center, near the subway that stopped right at our corner in Greenwich Village, so I could even get to Nan's by myself.

But as soon as we moved to New York, her health began to fail. Throughout high school, she was in the hospital many times after being diagnosed with a recurrence of cancer. The summer after my junior year, she had chemotherapy and most of her hair fell out. This was a major trauma, so my mother went out and got her a wig the next day. I went to see her the first day I arrived home from my summer in Italy, where I had been for six weeks on the Experiment for International Living. I had lived with families and had traveled all around the country where my two paternal grandparents had been born.

I had been warned about the hair, told to ignore the wig and pretend that she looked the same. She did not, but her hair looked pretty good, so I pretended not to notice. She was on to me, though, and she made me 'fess up to knowing about the wig.

"Come on!" she said. She looked straight at me with her hazel eyes wide open, then blinked three times for emphasis. "You cannot sit there and honestly tell me you can't tell." And she blinked again. So I told her that I had been warned, but that her hair truly did look good. I couldn't lie to my Nan; she had that way of staring you down. Her hair grew back pretty quickly and it was thicker and nicer than before.

By the following spring, however, she no longer cared about her hair. She was getting sicker, and there was nothing to be done about it. I remember the last time I went to the ballet with her, the winter before she really got sick. We saw the American Ballet Theater at the Metropolitan Opera House. It was so elegant there, with the chandeliers that rose up at the start of the program, the plush velvet seats, the smell of perfume in the air, and the mink coats all around. We saw a few short ballets that night; we loved those programs rather than the long story ballets, and I remember the first one had a Spanish feel with the ballerinas in stiff black tutus with red trim. I sat there next to Nan and felt an incredible sense of happiness. For a teenager, those moments can be few and far between, and I knew that. So I sat and savored the feeling. I was watching a great performance with my Nan. I had good friends and a good life and I did not dwell on what I lacked. I almost floated out of my seat that night. And the next morning when I woke up at Nan's bright apartment, I continued to feel good. We ate our bagels with sweet butter and drank our tea with milk and sugar before I went back to my house and my homework and my worries about boys and friends and parties.

We had Passover at Nan's that year. We did not usually celebrate the holiday, but my mother insisted that we have a seder at Nan's house. Nan was not very well and was wearing a dressing gown when we arrived. She must have been sick enough not to cook for us, since my mother brought the entire meal and much of the food was store-bought. My grandmother hated to spend money on prepared food and she was agitated at my mother for being so frivolous. They almost always had words about the amount of money my mother spent, on just about everything. My grandmother would walk two extra blocks in the cold, even when she was ill, to save ten cents on a quart of milk. I know this is true because I used to walk with her, offering to give her the dime from my own change if we could just get home. But she was headstrong. That night she lined up the food in the kitchen with the price tags showing so she could point out how much more my mother spent by going to the fancy Jefferson Market as opposed to the Fairway or the A&P. She had circulars out so she could show us how much less each item would have cost.

After this strange version of *The Price Is Right* was over, we got dinner ready. My mother wanted to do some of the religious components of the seder, and no one else was interested, least of all me. My father scoffed at her, my sister sighed heavily, Nan rolled her eyes indifferently, and I put up a fight. I could not be bothered with God, I said. There couldn't be a God, not after Steven and Ronnie. Not with Nan sick and nothing ever, ever going my way. I was sick of asking God for things and never getting them. I was tired of the deals and bargains that were one-sided at best. Usually I didn't even bother to hold up my side anymore. I had long known it was all a sham.

So I refused to participate. As my mother stumbled through a little Hebrew prayer and told Gina the story (my dad wasn't listening and Nan was still worrying about the cost of the meal), I looked out the window of Nan's living room. She had a view of the Hudson River and I could see across to New Jersey. The lights in the apartment buildings across the river sparkled, and the traffic on the West Side Highway flew by in a red and gold streak. I pressed my cheek against the coldness of the glass and vowed never to believe in God.

Two months later, while Nan was getting sicker by the day, my dog, Laffy, died. We went to school that morning knowing he was ailing, but we were sure that the vet could fix him right up. When we arrived home that afternoon, we were greeted by my father. He was never home in the middle of the day, and as soon as I heard his voice upstairs I knew the dog had died. We did not have time to cry, though. My mother was hosting a big, important party that evening, and Gina and I were to be there. She had bought us new dresses and shoes, and we were instructed to get dressed and get out the door. I don't really remember when we cried for our beloved pet, because soon after that, Nan died. We never even told her about the dog. She never asked, either. She was in and out of the hospital, and family members kept cycling through to help.

I was finishing my senior year of high school. I was supposed to be happy, carefree, and having fun for the last months of the spring. Instead, I was miserable. I was not ready for my grandmother to be so sick. I could not fathom that she was really dying. So I shut down to the situation. I stopped going to see her unless my mother made me go. Nan didn't seem to care who was there, anyway. I had gone to her house once that spring to bake a carrot cake. Her sister, Minnie, was there to help out. Minnie was a nurse, so she really could help, and Nan had wanted me to make her the cake. So I went over and baked it at Nan's house. But Nan didn't care about the cake. She could barely get out of bed, and when she did, I came into the room to say hi and she shooed me away. She was too sick; I was not to see her so ill.

The night before she died, she was in the hospital with a hired nurse to stay with her around the clock. My mother brought us to Sloan-Kettering Memorial Hospital to see her. I did not want to go, but I got in the car silently, and we drove uptown. I went into Nan's room, and she was lying in her bed, pale and asleep. She was actually in a coma, but I thought she was just sleeping. She did not stir when we came in. I did not get too close to her, did not touch her, or even really talk to her. I stood in the corner of the room for a few minutes until my mother told me to go to the TV room and wait for her there. I went down the hall and into the darkness of the TV room. I sat down without really looking around. It was a minute before I realized there was another person in the room. A patient, a cancer patient, was sitting in the chair next to the couch were I was sitting. He was about my age, thin and bald, and had tubes running in and out of him. I saw him and nodded at him before quickly gluing my eyes back to the TV screen. I did not look up again until his nurse came to get him. Then I looked up and nodded again at him. I may have given him a tiny, almost imperceptible smile before I reglued my eyes onto that screen. When my mother came to get me, I practically ran out of the room, out of the ward, out of the hospital. I told her about seeing the bald boy with the tubes.

"I didn't know that the TV room was for patients," I said with a note of panic in my voice.

"Oh, for God's sake," she said, "it isn't like cancer is contagious. I hope you talked to the guy; he's probably lonely in that hospital, you know."

Great, I thought as I got back into the car and we drove home. I'm supposed to chat amiably with the cancer patients while I wait for my grandmother to die. All I wanted to do was scream. People my age are not supposed to get cancer, and if they are sick, I don't want to see them. If I don't see them, I don't have to think about them, about them dying.

The next day was the last day of my senior year. The

phone rang while it was still dark outside. I heard my mother answer it and then I heard her footsteps on the stairs. I knew what she would say before she came into my room. Nan was dead.

I did not cry until a week later in the middle of my English exam. I started and could not stop. The family had already come and gone. The memorial service had been the Sunday before. After the service, many family members had spent the whole day at our house. My cousins were all there and so were many older relatives I did not know well. But I had been dry-eyed through everything. I wore the new shirt Mom had bought me for the fancy party (the day the dog had died), and we took photos of all the cousins together. I barely got through that English exam, which was required for me to graduate. Luckily, one of my teachers was passing by as I sat there, close to hysterical, and she got me to calm down by giving me some tissues and a roll of mints from her pocketbook.

I graduated from high school without my grandmother there. I had always imagined she would be there, but of course she was not. It was a year later that I felt her presence as I was waking up in my dorm room at Vassar. I missed her all the time and yet, since I was in a new place and in a new chapter of my young life, I was removed from missing her. Then, on this morning, I felt a flutter of air almost like a breath, a scent of the violet candies she kept by her bed, a brush of her fingertips on my cheek. When I opened my eyes, it was gone. I looked at the calendar. It was April 25, which would have been her seventy-fifth birthday.

I never thought about where she had gone when she died. I never thought about where any of the people (or my dog) who had died that year had gone. They were simply no longer here. There was no one in my family or in my circle of friends who told me that these dead people were now in heaven, in a better place, or looking down at me and smiling. No one said it was God's will or God's plan. Yet the feeling that my grandmother was with me on her birthday morning was a marvelous and happy feeling. Death was real and final, but through memory I could keep it from pulling me down. Sadness was tinted with sweetness when I thought of the people who were gone. Nan was not in heaven, I thought, but always in me, always near me. For as long as I had my memories of her, she stayed alive.

chapter 11

father daniel

Spirituality was not a part of my college experience. Not
unless there is a brand of spirituality that borders on self-
obsession. Because that is what I was: self-obsessed. And it
made sense, since this was my first real break from my
family. I was able to make many choices for myself for the
first time, like what classes to take, when to eat dinner, what
to eat, how late to stay out, and what to do in my free time.
No one was yelling at me to get out of bed at nine in the
morning, that the day was wasting and I ought to get up and
do something useful. No one was telling me to eat more vegetables, finish my chicken, and don't eat so many mashed
potatoes. If I wanted buttered noodles and pudding for
dinner, that was what I ate. If I showed up at ten-thirty for
breakfast and had two glasses of Tab and a bagel, no one
yelled at me to eat protein, and nobody nagged me that Tab
was going to kill me.

I loved being at college. I loved living on a small
campus and in a dormitory. It was all new and different for
me, coming from New York City. After having to take a
forty-minute subway ride to high school in Harlem, the ten-
minute walk through the bucolic countryside to my morning

psych class was a sheer pleasure. I had no idea school could be so pleasant, so pretty, so safe, and so much fun. I got to pick all my own classes, I had immediate pals due to the wonderful system of dorm living, and there was a bar right on campus, so I could go out without getting in a car, on a subway, or paying for cab fare.

My freshman year was a blur of classes, papers, parties, and new friends. I had many friends that first year, like my dorm pals Rick and Jennifer and, later, Sarah. I had my girl-friends, Annie and Laurie, and then I had the "Sluts," a ter-rible name for the great group of junior-year guys who played floor hockey together. They were like my big brothers. They did not live up to their name on or off the hockey floor, which is why it was so funny that they had such a name. My dorm was small and we were close. The friends I made there were the ones who really mattered. The people who were waiting for me "at home," those friends who were not part of the bar scene or the party scene, were the friends I really valued.

Rick and Jennifer were two of those friends. They did not like to go out to the campus bar, they did not care about seeing and being seen. They were upperclassmen, after all. Jennifer was a senior, with a serious boyfriend who had already graduated. She mostly studied and waited until she could have a weekend to go see Sean. Rick was a sophomore and had a girlfriend back at home. His high school sweet-heart was still in high school, and they were still a couple, although he was less than faithful. He did not have to ven-ture far to find a one-night stand, since there were many willing girls right in our dorm. And Rick never cared about the awkward meetings in the TV room afterward. He just ignored any tension and went on his way. He was from the South and had the whole southern gentleman thing working to his favor. He was never mean or dismissive, always polite; he was simply not willing to give much more than one or two nights.

Rick and Jennifer were never an item, and I was not interested in Rick (instead, I had my eye on the young man who had been Rick's freshman roommate). I met Rick in the first hours of college because I had been placed in "his" room—the room he had had as a freshman. I met Jennifer because she would come to Rick's cocktail parties, which he held in his room. He would lay out the gin, the vermouth, the ice bucket, and the glasses on a white towel and then mix martinis. I had one martini, once. I followed that with two gin and tonics, downed quickly because they tasted so weak compared to that first martini. I got so sick that Jennifer had to put me in my bed with my garbage can. I puked into it all night while the rest of the party checked in on me and continued to drink. I never had gin again. Sometimes, Jennifer and I would walk to the liquor store on a Friday afternoon and buy a bottle of Bailey's Irish Cream. We would drink that while Rick sipped his martinis. We poured it over ice and it was like an alcoholic milk shake.

Across the hall from Jennifer there was a senior girl named Karen. Karen was a prelaw student and seemed to study endlessly. I did not know her well, but Rick said she was cool and Jennifer seemed to like her. She was the Catholic Student Leader. I had no idea what that meant. I was only aware of the fact that we had a chapel on campus because I had drawn it in art class one evening. Apparently, we not only had a chapel, we also had a chaplain and other religious people who led services for students and professors at the chapel. After drawing the building, I actually went inside once to hear Reverend Jesse Jackson (during his campaign for president) and another time to listen to Timothy Leary (although I did not understand a word of what he said).

In the early spring, Karen invited us to come to the Catholic Student Association party. It was held off-campus, at the home of the priest who was associated with the chapel. I had my parents' car that semester, so we could drive. Karen said not to eat before, since there would be lots of food and a keg of beer, too. I was not really sure what to make of the idea of going to a Catholic priest's house to drink beer with my friends. It felt a little dishonest, like: "Oh, free beer. Okay, I'm a believer!" But Rick assured me that it would be a good party, that last year there had been great food, and that Father Daniel was a really cool, great guy. He had even left the priesthood for a while, which meant he was not some holier-than-thou type.

"Will it matter," I asked, "that I am a Jew?"

Rick just laughed at me. "I am sure that they'll check your head for horns at the door."

So we went to the party. It was not yet warm out and there were patches of snow clinging to the shady corners of buildings and in dirty clumps at the ends of parking lots. We piled into my car, with Rick at the wheel.

The family car was a 1972 Oldsmobile Cutlass Supreme. We had bought it new and even picked a "custom" color. I remember shopping for the car, weekend after weekend at car dealerships, because it seemed to take my parents forever to decide on a car. Then I remember the color chart they pored over. I loved that chart and all the shiny rectangles of colors with amazing names: sea-glass green, midnight blue, bing-cherry red. My parents finally picked antique gold, much to my disappointment. It was brown; we drove a brown car. I wanted one of those glittery beautiful colors. At least antique gold was glittery, even if it was brown. Eleven years later, the glittery color was pretty badly faded. The car was almost a relic; it was so huge and drove like a boat, sailing across the road with the enormous front end yawing out before you. If you floored the gas pedal, it really took off, though. You could even get it to fishtail and screech like in the 1970s cop shows on TV.

We got to the party early. We were hungry, since we had skipped the dining hall dinner. Father Daniel was there to greet us and he was not what I had expected. He was not wearing any kind of black uniform or even a collar. Instead, he was wearing blue jeans, a plaid shirt, and cowboy boots. This guy didn't look like a priest! And he didn't talk like one either. He was funny and told great stories. Many of them started with "During the years when I left the priesthood . . ." Father Daniel had left the priesthood at least once and for a period of many years. He had lived in New York City but had returned to the collar because he missed the work of the church.

The party was great. Many of the Catholic students were the wildest and most party-hearty on campus. Rick was chasing one girl, from our dorm, of course, who was the fastest and loosest girl I knew. She acted good and nice around Father Daniel at the beginning of the evening, but before long she was drunk and flirting shamelessly with the man. She was practically sitting on Father Daniel's lap, and at one point I thought she might drool into his beer.

I drank plenty of beer myself and ate some of the sandwiches from the kitchen table. They were from the best Italian deli in town; not as good as the ones from New York City, but not bad for Poughkeepsie. After we had been there for many hours, we got back into my car with the extra sandwiches Father Daniel made us take home. Rick swore that he was sober enough to drive and convinced me that we didn't have very far to go, in any case. I am sure he was weaving down the road, but we did get home safe. Perhaps Father Daniel had put in a good word for us with the big man upstairs.

I saw Father Daniel often after that. I had always wondered who he was around campus, and now I had another friend to say hello to as I walked from class to class or sat in the student center with my grilled cheese or plate of fries. I used to sit with him and chat at the student center. His clothing was always normal, the cowboy boots and jeans being a staple. He had red hair, a beard, and blue eyes—he looked very Irish. I liked the idea that I was pals with a priest. He knew my name, talked to me, and listened to me. I didn't talk about religion with him; I talked about classes, traveling, New York City, plans for the summer, things like that. I continued to run into him for the next year. I always wondered about him as a priest, like if he really believed in all the church stuff. He must have, he was a *priest* after all. But still, I thought, how can someone so normal be so holy?

Easter was a beautiful, warm day that year. In college, spring break was in early March, so we were back to school and in the final stretch of the classes before end-of-term exams came slapping us awake to the academic realities of college. Those warm spring Sundays were always spent wandering the campus, going from the library to the student center, over to the Art Building, then back to the dorm. It was as if I needed an excuse to be outside, and the restlessness gave me the reason I needed. Occasionally, I would haul my books out under a tree, but the ground was still damp from all the snow melting or the March rains. The best thing to do was to roam.

And on this particular Easter Sunday, I was doing just that when I realized it was Easter. I remembered that Passover had been the week before, because Mom had sent me a box of Passover candy—chocolate-covered coconut—which I had already eaten. I had seen signs posted around for the Jewish Student Seder, but I had not even thought of going. Aside from the forced seder at Nan's right before she died, the only other seder I had attended was the one my mom's friend Janet had taken me to when I was about ten.

She invited only me, so I was really excited. No mom and dad to shoot disapproving looks at me all night if I squirmed in my chair too much or if I asked too many questions. No little sister to get all the attention. I got dressed in my most grown-up outfit, the black dress with the little yellow flowers on it that had a sash, which my grandmother had sent me. Janet picked me up, and we walked over to her friend's house.

I had a grand time at the seder. I loved being the only kid; the adults all treated me as if I were one of them, they complimented my dress and had a seat for me at the table with them. Once the meal began, I was less thrilled to be there. There was a lot of talking before we got to eat, and the only thing we were allowed to have as a snack was some dry crackers, called matzoh. I liked matzoh at home; we bought it once in a while when Mom found it at the store, but we put butter and salt on it. There was no butter on the table and no salt either, so I nibbled at the tasteless matzoh while the grown-ups read from a book and talked and talked.

I did learn a few things that night. I learned that Jewish people had been slaves in Egypt and that a mean guy, named Pharaoh, treated them badly. But then another guy named Moses said, "Let my people go," and then the Jews ran away. They ran so fast that they forgot to make bread to eat for the trip, so they baked the dough that they had on the way, on rocks in the hot desert sun, while the army of the Pharaoh guy was at their heels. That was where the matzoh came from, from the rocks in the desert.

I also learned that getting invited to a seder was not such a great thing. We did finally eat, and I liked a few of the things that Janet's friend made for dinner, but it wasn't like I had gotten to go to McDonald's and have as many French fries as I had wanted. The only fun part for me was at the end, when I was instructed to find the matzoh. At the start of the dinner, there had been a piece of the cracker set aside, and now I was told to go find it. We needed that bit of cracker so everyone could eat it and we could go home. I was ready to go home, that was for sure, so I set off eagerly to find it. It wasn't hidden very well, and I found it almost immediately on the bookshelf behind the dinner table. Once I had it, they told me to sell it back to the host, which I did for two dollars. That was enough for a game of mini-golf at the mall, and I was quite content with my bargain.

After that seder, I did not need to go to another one. I was happy that there was no invitation from Janet the next year and that my mom ignored the holiday as usual.

I woke up that Sunday at Vassar vaguely recalling it was Easter but knowing it was fairly meaningless for me anyway. It had been years since my parents had hidden eggs and given me chocolate bunnies. At most, Easter was a day that we had to drive to the Bronx to my Italian grandmother's house, or to Westchester to my Aunt Jean's house. We often gathered for the holidays up there, since neither my aunt nor my grandmother liked to travel, even into Manhattan. I liked those trips, which usually included hanging out in the basement with my cousin Bill and playing pool, setting up race cars, or finding old family movies and watching them.

And then there was the food. My grandmother always made baked artichokes and fried zucchini, plus there was always an antipasto platter with sliced meats and roasted red peppers followed by baked ziti with sausage and meatballs. Then we would have roast chicken and green vegetables and maybe even potatoes. For dessert there was always a sideboard overflowing with cookies, the Italian kind made for Easter called *sfinci* and *cenci*. These were fried dough; the *cenci* in long strips and the *sfinci* in little balls that were doused in honey and powdered sugar. There was also Italian cheesecake and other assorted goodies. My grandmother always gave each grandchild a five-dollar bill at such occasions. I remember her pressing it into our hands, trying to avoid our protests of "No, Grandma! Don't give us your money!"

My mother complained bitterly about the holidays we spent in the suburbs. There was too much food, nowhere to walk, nothing to do; we just sat in the dining room all day. Once we decided to go to the Bronx Botanical Gardens to have an outing and please my mother. It was fun and we all liked it, but the next holiday we were back to sitting and eating.

As I wandered the campus that warm Easter of my freshman year, I thought again of the fact that this was a holiday and thought of my family and what they were doing. Gina was still living at home, so maybe they had gone up to the Bronx. I decided I would call later and find out. For now, though, I felt I should *do* something, something that was Easter-ish. I thought about what that meant, and I realized that after the food, Easter had very little significance to me at all. I knew that the real reason for the holiday was the resurrection of Jesus Christ. I knew that there was much at stake for the Christians around the world in this death and rebirth. This was a big-time, serious religious holiday that seemed incongruous with the happy little Easter Bunny, the chicks, and all that pink and yellow candy.

As I left the library and squinted into the sunlight, I decided to go to church. I knew that Father Daniel was giving a service at two o'clock because he had told me. It was one-thirty, just enough time to go get something to drink at the student center and get over to the chapel. I was properly dressed in my pink and gray striped skirt and white blouse, so I would not have to go back to my room. I met a guy from my dorm on my way to the student center and told him I was going to church. He was a Catholic, but was not going anywhere near church. He looked at me a bit strangely when I said that I thought church was just the place to go on Easter. Why, his look seemed to say, would you go to church unless your parents were dragging you there? I smiled at his confusion and walked in a very upbeat way to the student center. No one was there, so there was no one else to tell, "Hey, I'm going to church, me, the 'Jew'! What do you think of *that*?" And there was nobody else to drag along, either. So I went alone.

I wasn't alone when I got there. There were plenty of people filling the pews. There was music playing softly, and Father Daniel was up in front of all the rows of benches at the altar. Gone were his cowboy boots, jeans, and any semblance of "normal" appearance. He was wearing long brown robes tied with a ropelike belt, and on his feet were sandals. My jaw almost dropped. This did not look like the same guy. When the service began, my confusion deepened. He really was a priest; he was all about Christ and God and the Holy freaking Host. I felt myself recoiling, almost in horror. Oh, he didn't say anything scary, not like those crazy, ski-trip Christians. He was only being a priest, after all. And that was his job, his calling, his true passion. The religion, the scripture, the sermons, and the Communion were what he was really all about. All those cups of coffee and small-talk chats were part of him, too, I guess. Just like anyone else, he could leave work aside and just chat, you know, to be social. But as I sat there listening to the deeply religious talk and prayer, as I watched the people sing with their heads bowed and line up for Communion, I felt like a complete outsider. I didn't know what to do, or when to do it. I didn't want to bow my head, I could never take Communion, and I simply did not belong there. I wanted to stand up and yell, "Let me out! I made a mistake! I cannot sit here!" But of course, I sat there and waited for the Easter service to end so I could get back outside into the sunshine and the fresh spring air, back out to where I belonged.

The service ended with the handshake of peace. You had to stand up and shake hands or even hug the people around you. This was a horrifying moment for me, because it meant I had to make eye contact and skin contact with all these strangers. Even if I knew some of the people in the pews near me—and I did, because Vassar was a small campus—and although most people were at least familiar by sight, I certainly did not know them in a church context. And I felt sure they would be able to tell that I was an interloper, a nonbeliever. So I gritted my teeth as I shook one and then another person's hand. And I mumbled, "Peace," just like they were doing. Then it was over.

On my way out, I went to say hello to Father Daniel. He seemed surprised to see me there, and I laughed it off: "What else would a good Jew do on Easter?" I said. He made some jokes about his brown robes and said that the sandals were remarkably comfortable. I was relieved to be speaking to Father Daniel as I usually did, but something in me had shifted. It was almost as if I couldn't trust him now, even though he wasn't trying to convert me. I did remain friends with Father Daniel until he left the campus for other work in the Catholic church. But I never tried to go to church at Vassar again.

chapter 12

agnosticism in italy

my junior year of college was divided in half: the first half was spent at college where nothing seemed to go right, and the second half was my semester abroad, in Florence, Italy. I was an Italian major (actually I was a double major, Italian and fine art), so it was academically acceptable for me to go to Italy. I had loved my trip to Italy in high school and had majored in Italian with the idea of going back someday, since I had loved the food, the people, and the beautiful cities. Plus, I was "Italian," since my paternal grandparents had been born there.

My parents' marriage was falling apart, and although they tried to keep it from me, the late-night calls from my mother (who was either drunk or distressed) were a sure sign that all was not well. I also knew, from my sister who still lived at home, that my mother had taken to sleeping in my room and that she and Dad were barely speaking most of the time. I already had some distance from the family, since I had been at Vassar for two years, and I knew I would be leaving for my six months in Italy right after Christmas. So there were plenty of distractions from the domestic problems of a house that was seventy-five miles away.

In October of my junior year, I had all four of my wisdom teeth taken out on a sunny morning. I remember going into the room, breathing some gas, and then waking up slumped against a wall and throwing up. I spent a week in bed recovering. I took pain medication and watched soap operas. I was home for a total of ten days, and although my parents were barely speaking, I was delirious enough to think that they would work it all out. My sister tried to dispel me of this notion, hissing at me: "They are putting on a show for *you.*"

I returned to school relieved to be back in my college cocoon. Making up for work I had missed and going to parties occupied my first week back. Two weeks later, my best friend suffered a nervous breakdown and left school. Sarah had stopped going to classes weeks before and had not gotten out of bed except to get drunk or buy more cigarettes in all that time. Then one day she decided that it would be best to just go home. And so I helped her pack her room and drove her to catch the minibus to the airport. Once she got home, things got worse, and she called many times in the month of November threatening to hurt herself. Rick and I spent hours on the phone with her, and we finally called her father to alert him to the situation. She was obsessing over a boy who had left her for his hometown girl, and was desperate to get him back. None of her efforts paid off; she never did get Al to leave the other girl and she lost friends in her crazy attempts to win him. Rick and I were exhausted by her after a while and we had to stop taking her calls.

The day before Thanksgiving, a girl from my hall was killed in a car accident. I had seen her as she left the dorm to go to her fieldwork job north of Poughkeepsie. We had stopped and chatted and had made plans to see each other in the city. I still had one paper to hand in, although it was already four hours late and I was scrambling to get it to my political science teacher before another hour ticked by and I lost another third of a grade.

Lisa was dead by three o'clock that afternoon. Lisa and I had been on the same floor in the same dorm for two and a half years. We had never been best buddies but had always made time to meet for a tea or to see each other over holidays in the city. She was a smart, funny, talented girl who sang with an a cappella group on campus. I loved going to the concerts and always liked seeing her sing. And now, just hours after I had seen her leave the dorm, she was dead.

The family held a memorial service one Saturday afternoon before the final exam period began. It was so sad. When I told her mom that I might have been the last person to see her that day, she hugged me and thanked me for telling her everything Lisa had said, everything she had done, what she had been wearing, what time it was . . .

I left for Christmas emotionally exhausted and relieved to be getting a break from school. Since I was not returning to campus the following semester and I had packed my room, there were now three empty rooms on the hall: mine, Sarah's, and Lisa's. As I said good-bye to many friends who would graduate while I was gone, I realized that I would come back to a different place. I drove to the city in a rented station wagon with all my possessions in the back. I was ready to get home and pack for my three months in Italy. I arrived to a house in disorder. My parents were miserable. My sister was angry and rebellious. My father took me to dinner to tell me that he was moving out. Then he left for Christmas in Rome without us.

My mother, Gina, and I went to Vermont for a cold and dismal Christmas. We arrived at the rented cabin late at night with my cousins, having ridden the seven freezing hours in the backseat of their tiny car. We met my mother's sister, Aunt Leila, there and tried to act like a happy family. Everyone else went skiing, but I stayed back at the ugly ski cabin, alone. I read D. H. Lawrence novels and baked chocolate chip cookies, which I burned. So instead of the usual assortment of nut balls, sugar cookies, and pinwheels that I baked each Christmas with Mom and Dad, I was scraping the burned part off the Toll House cookies and blinking back tears. By the end of the week, we were all sick with winter colds and could hardly swallow because our throats were so sore. On the trip home, Mom, Gina, and I passed the medicine around as if we were three hobos sharing a bottle of Thunderbird. I arrived home only to pack and leave for my three months in Florence a few days after the New Year.

I arrived in Florence on a cold and snowy day. It was an unusually cold winter in Europe that year. After a few days, my throat finally stopped feeling as if an ice pick was running though it each time I swallowed. I was staying in a little *pensione* for the first two weeks, but I really wanted my own apartment. I found one with a roommate named Maureen, who was another American student from my language program. We moved into a villa on the south side of Florence. The one-bedroom apartment was small, but we lived in the middle of a garden on a tree-lined street that was lovely and quiet, close enough to school that we could get there by bus or a twenty-minute walk. The landlord had only wanted to rent to girls, and he thought we were acceptable because we seemed well bred. Mr. Canto was a real

Florentine snob. He claimed to be related to Machiavelli, but it turned out that almost all wealthy Florentines say they are related to Machiavelli.

The best thing about being in Florence was that Deborah was there, too. We had been best friends in high school and remained close even though she was in college in Boston. She lived on the north side of Florence, so by foot we were more than an hour away, but a bus connected our houses in fifteen minutes. Usually, we would meet in the center of town, since she went to an art school near my language school. Her classes were all in English, and she had many artsy classmates. I could not speak English anywhere in the school I attended and I was the only art major in the group. Most of the others were language or art history majors.

I had classes all morning, all in Italian. I would get to school by nine o'clock, having consumed three coffees on the way. After buzzing through my classes, it was lunchtime. Deborah's school was just a few blocks away from mine, and we were always seeing each other for lunch, usually at ZaZa's near the central market. We would meet at her school because I liked the smell of oil paint and seeing all those art students who were always working on cool projects. We would go around the corner to get a seat at one of the long tables at ZaZa's. After a big bowl of pasta and a half liter of wine, we would need a *caffé* to get us to our next class or to my studio.

I had agreed to come to Florence with the Middlebury Program, provided they got me a studio so I could do an independent painting course for my fine art major. At first there was no studio, so I was unhappy with no place to paint. I had brought all my supplies, but my apartment was too small and the oil paints I used were too smelly. And Mr. Canto would hate it if I painted in his villa. I would stay at Deborah's school all afternoon sometimes, just wishing I had a place like that to work in. Finally, I went to the director of my school and cried—literally wept—out of frustration with not having a studio space. The next week, she arranged for me to rent a corner of an artist's studio to use as my space. The artist, Senor Colaccechi, was the son of a well-known painter and was carrying on for the old man. I almost never saw either of the men, but I loved the studio. It was in the north part of town, not far from where Deborah lived. It was in an old building that seemed to always have been an artist's studio and had a courtyard and a window so large it opened with a crank. The studio itself was huge, and my corner was great. There was another girl who had rented the opposite corner, but she was almost never there. I had that whole place to myself most afternoons.

So after lunch, I would head over to the studio, stopping at the little coffee bar on the corner for my *caffè corretto*, espresso coffee with a shot of Sambuca. Then it was off to work until it started to get dark. I painted every day while I had that studio, dreadful paintings of figures from my imagination or dreamlike scenes. I used bright colors, looking at Matisse or the German expressionists; anyone other than Italian Renaissance painters. The whole time I lived in Florence, I longed for a modern art museum that I could visit. "Modern" in Italy meant the 1800s. I went to the Uffizi and the Palazzo Pitti, but the paintings were not what I wanted to see. I did not care for all the Madonna paintings, the Crucifixions, or the Annunciations.

Oh, sure, I appreciated all the art. I loved all the

museums and the churches and all the old stuff all around me. But I wanted a direct emotional connection to the art and I was not getting it from the Renaissance. The stuff in the museums and churches all seemed too old-fashioned, too beautiful, and too religious. I wanted angst and fear, people, not Gods, and color that was saturated and high-contrast. I wanted to look at paintings that reflected the modern human condition so I could relate them to my modern life. And how on earth did all those mothers and children or dead guys on crosses relate to me?

While I was in Italy, my parents did separate. The night I realized Dad had moved out of the house on 12th Street was a cold, dark night in February. I had gotten a message at school from my sister and I called home from the post office in Piazza Repubblica on my way to my apartment. After talking to Gina for a few minutes, I wanted to speak to Dad, but he was at work. So I waited to place the second call to his office. He was there, and I was very happy to hear his voice. He sounded sad and far away. He had his own apartment on 34th Street, he said, and all was well. I hung up wishing I could believe that.

I walked home slowly in the cold, darkening evening. I vaguely recalled that my roommate had invited some friends over. By the time I got all the way home, I was late for dinner, but I didn't care. I was not in the mood for people in my little apartment. I entered the apartment in the middle of dinner and went straight through the first room into our bedroom. I got into bed and turned on the tiny TV we had, which got one channel in Italian, and that night the only thing on was *Charlie's Angels*. The fuzzy picture came and went, and the dubbed dialogue was difficult to follow considering that my mind was elsewhere. After a while, some of Maureen's guests (they were my friends, too, but that night I had to think of them as her guests) came in to check on me. This antisocial behavior was way out of character for me. I reluctantly turned off the TV and came out into the party. After a glass of wine, I ended up teary-eyed and had to tell them all why I was so upset. I sort of ruined the festive mood, but I did feel better sharing my family secret: that I had divorced parents. So did almost everyone else in the room, though, and so I got some much-needed story swapping and tales from the battlefront. Some of my friends were surprised that I had such a thing going on at home, since I had failed to mention it in all the weeks we had been together.

I walked around after that in a strange mood. I wore my Walkman everywhere, listening to Elvis Costello wailing or the Style Council lamenting. I felt alone and isolated, even in a crowded restaurant with all my friends. And I felt even worse when I passed churches. Being an agnostic in a strongly Catholic country was hard work, because when I passed the churches I felt guilty that I did not go inside and find solace. Since the possibility of God's existence nagged at me, since I still harbored the hope that he would intervene on my behalf in some aspect of my miserable life (family, love, grades), I was always feeling that I should go into one of the hundreds of churches. But I never did go into any of the churches in Florence. There was no candle I could light to take my troubles away. There was no prayer I could say to help make me feel better. The images of Jesus did not make me feel warm and loved.

When I say I did not go into the churches of Florence, I mean I did not even enter any of them, not even to see the masterpiece works of art. I knew there were hundreds of paintings, sculptures, altarpieces, and objects within the walls of the sacred domains that dot the Italian cities and towns. I had studied art history and was taking a Renaissance art class. It was at nine o'clock in the morning on Thursdays and it was in Italian, so I was usually dozing or completely confused by the language. I knew all the names, of course: Botticelli, Cimabue, Duccio, Giotto, Fra Angelico, Verrocchio. But to see the work meant entering the churches. And I just didn't go.

I meant to go. I did not realize that I was making a statement by not going. I usually planned to go but ended up at my studio instead, painting on one of my confrontational figures, someone contemporary, often a self-portrait or a figure from my own invention. That was far more interesting and a more important use of my time as an artist, I figured. I needed to paint, to express myself, and how were all those musty-dusty things in churches going to help me? It was not that I was arrogant, since I knew I was in need of help as a developing artist, but I did not want it from the art that was all around me. Instead, I pored over the book from the Museum of Modern Art that I had brought with me and longed to go see Vuillard and Bonnard back at the museum in New York City. I wanted to see work that focused on the little moments of life as it is now. I would have given up all the art in Florence to see one room of Matisse: secular, colorful, flat, and modern.

Deborah caught on. She was an art history major and went into all the churches. She was as non-Christian as I was.

"Nica," she would ask me, "have you gone to Santa Croce?"

"No."

"Have you been to Santa Maria del Carmine?"

"Not yet."

"Let's go to Rome—what churches won't Nica go to there?"

I never even went inside Santa Maria del Fiori, the largest church in the city, until May. I finally visited the Duomo, as it is called because of its famous and mysterious dome (no one knows how the architect, Brunelleschi, got it to stay up), when my father visited me. He had wanted to see something inside, and I was happy to go along. Up until then, I did not avoid going, I just did not think of doing it on my own. I *had* gone into the tiny church of Santa Felicità with Deborah once; she was doing a paper on the painter Pontormo, so I went in with her to see the mannerist paintings of the elongated Madonna and stretched-out saints.

Dad stayed for a week and we had a great time. We spent a few days in Florence and then rented a car and drove to Pisa and Portofino for a long weekend. I had my final exam in art history in June, after Dad left. The final was an oral exam, all in Italian, of course. Professor Ercole looked the part of the art historian; he wore brown checked jackets with elbow patches and had glasses that perched on the end of his long nose. He had white hair and sat up very straight with his hands folded in front of him; this exam was serious business. Not only did I have to answer all his questions about the Renaissance correctly, I had to do it in perfect Italian. An hour before it was my turn to go, I ran into a fellow student.

"He asked where the paintings are!" she told me.

"Well, that's easy—they are all here in Florence," I said happily. Maybe I could ace this test I had barely studied for after all.

"No." she said. "Which churches, you have to remember which church each piece is in! I almost died but I think I got them all."

"Yeah," I said as I gulped. "That's great."

"Good luck!" she yelled over her shoulder. "*Buona fortuna!*"

What could I do? With fifty-five minutes until my exam, I could not race around to all the churches. I opened the book I had for the class. The captions for the paintings told the city, but not always the church for each piece, plus not all the paintings we had studied were in the book. I was screwed. I got a coffee at my usual standup café around the corner from school and resigned myself to the fact that I would fail the course, and the grade would not transfer to my transcript. I would have to make up the credit at some point; I'd probably ruin my senior year with an overload of classes.

I went into the room for the exam feeling nervous from the double *caffé* I had just downed but calm when it came to answering the questions. What could I say? I did not know and would not know the specific locations of the works of art. And I had only myself to blame for being unmotivated to go into churches. When the professor held up one after another of the pictures from class, I had to guess where they were. I got a few guesses right, but in the end, he asked me why I had not visited the churches.

"I did visit the Duomo," I told him.

"Ah, good, then which of these did you see there?" He flipped through a few of the books in front of him and produced several horse-and-rider paintings.

I pointed to one I thought I had seen there, or maybe it had been in my book. "I did not really look at the paintings,"

I said, as I became sure I had pointed to the wrong painting. "I am so much more interested in the architecture."

This lame lie got me a C, all I needed for the grade to transfer as a "pass" onto my college transcript. Later that day, I paused in front of the huge and beautiful Duomo. I sat on the steps and felt relief that the exam was over, that my semester was finished. Our grades had been announced to us as we left the school for the day, so I did not have to wait for the grade to be mailed to me. I could enjoy the relief right then and there.

As I sat there, I thought about how far I had come from the lowest point of my stay. I thought about the dark, cold winter evenings when I felt alone and far away from everything. I thought about the isolation I felt as my family fell apart and friends forgot to write. I remembered the day I wanted to go home. Deborah and I had run into each other in Piazza Repubblica and had gone to Gilli for hot chocolate with whipped cream. I started the afternoon convinced I would leave and go home to deal with my parents' breakup and fix all the problems I had left behind. I ended the day deciding to stay, of course, and found fresh resolve to try to be happy while I was in Italy.

Now I felt I was happy. I looked around at the throngs of tourists, Florentines, and other American students wandering through the center of town. I felt as if I belonged in that little city, because I had managed to make myself a life there. I looked up at the colored marble façade of the Duomo with the red, green, and gray marble, the sculptures, the mosaics, and beautiful doors, and I got up and went inside. After my eyes adjusted, I looked at all the interior had to offer. And I really looked this time. There was the horse and rider from the test; I had chosen the correct one after all! I sat down under the great dome and took a deep breath. I was not the same as the day I had arrived in Florence. I had not found faith in the churches, but I had found faith in myself. I could sit in the church and not be afraid that I would be marked as a nonbeliever. I stood up and walked back out into the beautiful June sunshine. I looked around the piazza. I felt it was mine; the whole city was mine. I had come with my trunk on a bleak January morning and here I was, six months later. I hadn't been defeated by the winter or the loneliness. I was far away from my family and many of my friends, and yet I felt a confidence, a security, and a sense of place.

As I made my way home to New York City, via Paris and London, I realized that the sense of belonging in a place was within me. It did not matter what city I was in, I could be myself in any one of them. I was ready to go home and face the uncertainty of the life I had left behind. I was sure I could belong there as I had learned to belong in Florence.

part 2

chapter 13

my sister is a christian

I came home from my European stay and found that much
had changed in New York. Although I knew my parents had
separated, it was not until I walked in the front door of our
house that the reality hit me. The house was almost unrecog-
nizable. My father had taken some of the furniture, and my
mother had moved her business into the second floor, so the
house seemed empty yet chaotic. I helped my mother start to
get things back into shape as soon as I slept off my jet lag.
We moved furniture and organized things for a few days
before I could be there without a feeling of panic taking over.

After a week of working on the house with Mom, I got
a job and tried to reconnect with my old friends. I had been
away for six months, and some of the friendships to which I
thought I would return were no longer there. The hole my
absence left had filled up, and I felt extraneous. I had a
birthday party for myself in mid-August and ended up
feeling that I had not really wanted to see very many of the
guests—my supposed pals. I was eager to get out of New
York and get back to college: Vassar had always belonged to
me. I had no family ghosts to honor or obey on campus; it
was only my own history there that might haunt me.

My senior year I lived in a town house, which was a nice word for an ugly prefabricated house owned by the college. Five students lived in each town house, and the houses were a ten-minute walk away from the main part of campus. Our town house had been assembled by my friend Ellen while I was in Italy. I lived in the lone downstairs room, while Ben, Mike, Greg, and Ellen had the upstairs rooms. I had been looking forward to living in the house all summer. I knew it would be a fun group of people and I was happy to be able to cook my own meals instead of enduring another year of cafeteria food. I would not have to live on buttered noodles and wilted salad anymore, nor the pizzas, grilled cheese sandwiches, or French fries that made up for meals that had been too terrible to face.

I had been happy to pack up my room midyear and get on a plane. I had been eager to get away from the smallness of campus life. But now I was ready to start fresh after my break. I had a new, worldly perspective, was more confident, and was top dog, a senior. I felt this was my last chance to enjoy college and everything that a small, insular campus had to offer: friends at the ready, the college center with the snack bar and social scene, the libraries open until late, and the natural beauty of the campus. And I was ready to focus on my art major. I wanted to get my studio set up and get to work painting. I wanted to continue to focus on figures. In Italy I had worked from my head, inventing people to keep me company in my secluded studio. Now that I was back on campus, I thought I would get real people to sit for me. I was excited to use my friends as models and to work on a large scale.

All five of the housemates had agreed to arrive early to

set up our house, but Greg was the last to get there. He had the farthest to come, since he was from California. He drove the whole way each year, in his powder-blue Ford truck. I didn't know Greg very well, aside from always recognizing his truck around campus, but I was eager for him to get there. He was a good-looking, quiet guy, but I sensed there was something under the calm exterior. All week Ben, Ellen, Mike, and I hung around and got the house set up. We went to KMart or Shop-Rite and kept a lookout for Greg. It was almost dark that Thursday before we saw him. Mike, Ellen, and I were playing Frisbee (very badly) on the field outside our house, while Ben was inside "decorating."

Ben arrived with boxes of maps, ads, pictures, and even empty cereal boxes that he stapled onto the walls of the house. Slowly our house became like a Kurt Schwitters Environment, with every wall covered. Once, Ben even glued a chair to the kitchen ceiling. I finally had to lock my staple gun away. But that did not stop Ben; he just switched to glue, tape, or old chewing gum. To some it looked like a garbage dump. To us it was a fun-filled activity, except when it got out of hand. Once, in an "out of hand" episode, Ben filled Greg's room with wadded-up newspaper. Another time he nailed hot dogs all over Ellen's room (she was the resident vegetarian). But mostly Ben kept it interesting and lighthearted.

With Greg there, the house was complete. Within a few days of his arrival, I realized that I liked him, *liked him* liked him. This was madness! At Vassar you could not get serious with a housemate. You were not really supposed to date anyone; you were supposed to sleep around and not care if those one-night stands ever spoke to you or looked your way again. I had not been happy with those game rules, yet I was unsure what would happen if I broke them, especially with a housemate.

Greg and I were spending more and more time together, and after a few weeks of being inseparable, we realized that we should just "go out." The funny thing was that we didn't really go anywhere, we liked hanging out at home or driving around campus in the truck. He was an all-American, small-town guy. I was intrigued by his California upbringing, his conservative family, and his stories of salmon loaf with three-bean salad. I was amazed that he had come so far from home for college. While I had driven two hours to get to school, he had driven four days. I had the sense that the distance was part of an escape for him. I got a peek of what he left behind when his sister came through for a quick visit later in September.

Megan and her boyfriend, Jed, were driving from Rochester, New York, to Manhattan. They had graduated the June before from music school and were to begin master's studies in the city. He was a jazz guitar player and she was a classical pianist. Greg had brought a bedroom set from California in the back of his truck for Megan, and she was picking it up from Vassar.

Greg warned us that his sister was different from anyone we knew at Vassar. He said that she and her boyfriend would sleep over, but that they wouldn't sleep *together*. None of us could understand what he meant. How could they be going out and not sleep together?

"Well, you see, my sister is a Christian," Greg answered with a straight face. "She doesn't believe in premarital sex."

I thought Greg was kidding. I had never met anyone who

was "saving themselves" for marriage. I knew people who identified themselves as belonging to a religion and even went to church. But no one I knew was so pious that they would not sleep in the same bed as a boyfriend or girlfriend. Sarah, my old dorm friend, had called herself a Mormon. She declared it often, usually as she took a drag off her cigarette or poured herself another drink from the many bottles she kept in her room. When she got a visit from a fellow Mormon during her sophomore year (she said that is what Mormons do, they visit other Mormons who are away from home to see if they are doing well and staying in the church), we had to move all the alcohol, all the cigarettes and ashtrays, the Coke and Pepsi bottles, and the coffeemaker into my room. That way she could get a good report and not upset her parents. That night we got drunk, and she stayed in her boyfriend's room. She was certainly not going to let religion stand in the way of a good time.

I met Megan and Jed the next morning, since they had arrived late the night before. I emerged from my first-floor bedroom to see two sleeping bags on the foldout couch. They were not zipped together but rather remained separate. I chuckled to myself as I went into the bathroom to brush my teeth. I made coffee, and pretty soon the house was up. We gathered in the kitchen around a drab brown table in front of the sliding glass door. Ben's decorating was the only thing of interest in the room, and our guests eyed all the stapled stuff with skeptical curiosity.

The sister and her boyfriend seemed nice enough. Megan was small and had a high-pitched voice; she looked like her brother—the same light skin with dark hair and eyes. Jed was quiet, he wore glasses, had a beard, and was rather tall. We had coffee together, and then I left for class. By the time I came back, they were pulling out with the bedroom set in the back of the station wagon they had borrowed from Jed's parents for the move to the city. I noticed then that the bedroom set was the kind with two twin beds.

I took Greg home to meet my parents for Thanksgiving. We went to Dad's new apartment the night before Thanksgiving. Dad cooked an enormous dinner, and we had a great time. Dad was glad to meet Greg, and the two seemed to get along right away. Then we spent the next few days with my mom. She liked Greg, too, but only after doing an interview with him the first morning we were home. We had slept in my room, of course. My mother had never cared about premarital sex or saving oneself for marriage. In fact, she had always offered our house as a "safe house," a place to bring your boyfriend, for anyone whose parents were more strict or old-fashioned. She didn't exactly grill Greg, but she did ask him a lot of questions about his hometown, his parents, and his upbringing. By the end of the weekend, she and my new boyfriend were pals and she had invited his whole family to come to New York anytime.

By the end of the first semester of our senior year, Greg and I were pretty serious, so I flew to California to see Greg for part of the winter break. I was eager to meet Greg's family, but I was nervous, too. Greg had assured me that no discussion of religion or politics would come up with his family, since they were too "polite" to bring up anything that might lead to disagreement or discord. Unlike my mother's interrogative techniques, Greg's mom would not ask me anything other than what kind of chocolate cake I liked best. I knew he had told her about me, my family, what I looked like, and that I didn't go to church. But still, I wondered if she would like me, or if I would be too different from her and her family in too many ways. My ethnic background might clash with their Waspy heritage. And what if religion did come up? Greg's whole family went to church, and they might be uncomfortable with me coming from a "Jewish" family, or worse, perhaps, being nothing.

Plus, my parents were divorced, and that *never* happened in Greg's family. Unfortunately, however, I would not be meeting Greg's father, who had committed suicide the October of Greg's freshman year at Vassar. He dropped Greg off at college, flew back home, then a few weeks later checked himself into the hospital only to leave and jump off a highway bridge. The family was still reeling from the loss, but they were really good at acting as if nothing was wrong.

I arrived late on a Saturday night and was shown to the guest room. Greg and I practically lived in his room at school, but the house rule under his mother's roof was separate bedrooms. Early the next morning, before I got up, his family left for church. Greg didn't have to go, so I didn't have to go either. I had feared his mom might decide that we had to go after all, so I was relieved that we really did not have to go.

Greg had stopped going to church years ago. In fact, he had never really liked going to church. He started asking his parents if he could skip it when he was six or seven. They would not allow such dissension; the family went to church and Greg was part of the family, end of discussion. One Sunday, when Greg was in first grade and was again denied a reprieve from the torture of church, he decided to take action. He stole his father's cigarette lighter and went into the bathroom during Sunday school. His plan was to set some paper towels on fire, thinking that if the church burned then he would no longer have to be there every week. But when he reached into the pocket of his Sunday pants, the lighter was gone. Greg was sure that God had intervened and kept his house from flames (the same way I had felt after lying and then ending up with a blood blister). Months later, while Greg's dad was cleaning out the station wagon, the lighter resurfaced. It had fallen out of Greg's pants pocket and slid down the crack in the backseat. Greg was frozen in his tracks when his dad held up the lighter, saying, "Oh, look! That's where it got to. I've been looking for this!" Greg's brief period of belief evaporated at that moment and never came back.

Greg and I had a great time in California, and as it turned out, I really liked his mom, Arlene. She liked to laugh and sit around the table and talk. In the whole week I was there, we chatted and chatted but never said anything even vaguely provocative. It was clear she was a conservative Republican, she loved Reagan as her president, and she told me that Nixon was innocent. I was trying to avoid any conflict in keeping with Greg's family, so when she said that, I nodded, smiled, and then changed the subject. As for the whole religion discussion, it never came up. We all seemed to avoid it, and so nothing was asked and nothing was divulged. I was glad that there had been no demanding questions or challenges made about my beliefs by any of Greg's family. But it seemed strange to me that during the whole trip, nobody ever asked me any questions at all about my family or our religion. I was not used to the nonconfrontational way of Greg's clan, but I was learning that it was easier to leave hard topics unprobed.

As much as I liked Arlene and the rest of Greg's family, the differences between my family and theirs were obvious, if unspoken. I realized this most clearly when I was asked to help out in the kitchen making "sweet potato balls" that had marshmallows in the middle. They were pretty good, even though in my family marshmallows were for roasting on a camping trip, and my parents had never served them with sweet potatoes. In fact, my parents shopped every day, and we never bought meat from a supermarket. They stopped at the butcher counter and got only what we needed for that night. Our freezer had vodka, ice cream, and some frozen peas in it at any given time.

But Greg's family was traditional, an American cuisine kind of a family, and that meant all kinds of bottled salad dressings on the table, frozen foods, and store-bought desserts. Plus they cooked with ingredients like mayonnaise and Velveeta. They lived in the middle of the agricultural capital of the state, the salad bowl of America, yet "salad" to them was canned beans and frozen corn with bottled Italian dressing. Sometimes the salad was even pink, some sort of Jell-O and cranberry concoction (with more marshmallows, this time the mini variety). When that was served, everyone kept asking me to pass the salad, but I didn't know what they were referring to; I saw no green on the table. The bowl of pink next to me never registered in my mind as salad. Greg finally reached across me to pass the bowl.

Greg didn't like pink salad either and he had even less patience for his family's religion. But he, like the rest of his family, was good at avoiding the topic. Clearly that was a family specialty. Without ever talking about it, somehow Greg's family accepted him for who he was, even as an

atheist. Maybe they saw his distance from the church as
temporary, maybe they thought that he would come back to
the church someday. He didn't ever show a sign of
budging, didn't offer to go to church "for old time's sake,"
and didn't bow his head during prayer before dinner the
way his sister did.

When Megan (who was also home from school) was at
the table, grace was said with some solemnity and length.
And even though my head was bowed, my eyes were open
and I could sneak a peek at her face. She was rapt and really
praying. I was amazed that she was so concentrated on this
moment of supposed communion with God. Was she really
talking to him? Was he really listening? It was strange to me
that she not only spoke to God, right there at the dinner
table, but that she followed all the rules he had supposedly
laid out. I thought again of the twin beds and the saving-
myself-for-marriage idea that it symbolized. Was that really
a rule, I wondered? Did the Bible really say, explicitly, thou
shalt not have sex before marriage? Was she trying to please
God the same way she would be trying to please a really
strict father?

I ended up catching Greg's eye by the end of the
predinner prayer, and we smiled tiny, conspiratorial smiles
at each other. No matter how Christian his sister was, Greg
was the guy for me.

chapter 14

living in sin

The second half of senior year was a frenzy of seminar papers, painting constantly for my senior show, and trying to move to Boston. Greg was a psychology major, and I was a fine art major, so neither of us had to write a thesis. (I dropped the Italian major once I returned from Italy; I loved the language and the country but I was not going to be able to study Dante and had no interest in reading the literature from the seventeenth century.) That left us some time during the spring for looking at apartments in Boston. Greg and I chose Boston because we did not want to be like every other Vassar graduate and move to New York City. My whole family was in New York, and I wanted to strike out on my own, even if it was just a few hours north on the East Coast. Greg and I never thought of living in separate apartments, and, since we had already been housemates, there was no stress of moving in together. It made perfect sense that we would pool our limited resources and get an apartment to share.

We found an apartment in a part of town that was near lots of nice neighborhoods, but the immediate area around our building was pretty nasty. The apartment we rented was nice enough; it had clean wood floors and a new kitchen even if it did overlook a filthy parking lot and the stairwells smelled of rotting food and dirty diapers. After we paid our first month of rent in August, we had about ten dollars between us for the rest of the week. We were working, but until that Friday's paycheck, we had to live on pasta, rice, and whatever canned food we had in the house.

Our first jobs didn't really have anything to do with our studies at Vassar. Greg was working as a private investigator, and I worked as an extended day teacher in the suburbs. So we were the spy and the teacher, except that Greg was telling all our friends that he worked as a management consultant (whatever that was). But really he was working undercover as a suit salesman in a high-end outlet store. He drove an hour each way to work and had to lie about where he lived, what his background was, and everything else about his life. Once at work, he sold suits to bargain hunters and acted as if he really cared about his career path and was even promoted while he was there. What he was really trying to do was catch some employee who was ripping off millions of dollars in store merchandise, so he posed as the gung-ho salesman and took notes on all the other employees. Sometimes, when there was nothing suspicious to report, he would "tell" on his fellow workers if they took too long at lunch or snuck a cigarette break in the back of the store. He did eventually help catch the assistant manager who was dealing in stolen suits. After that assignment, he worked nights at a computer storage facility where there were drug dealers who needed to be ratted out. Plus he often had "little" jobs, like digging through people's garbage or following someone for days.

I had to commute every day too and I drove the blue truck to and from the suburban town of Lexington. The powder-blue truck was too unusual a color for Greg to drive, so he borrowed his sister's normal-colored car for the year. I liked working in a school and I liked the hours, plus I had some mornings free so I could do my artwork. But I never really liked the commute; I was forever worried about the weather, and after I had car trouble one time, I became afraid of the truck exploding under me.

Christmas of that year, we hosted Greg's mom and his sister in our apartment in Boston. I was nervous about having Greg's family in the apartment Greg and I shared in sin. We had a bedroom and a double bed, of course. His family knew that we were a couple and that we slept together, but I knew they did not approve. Greg and I had slept in two separate parts of the house at his mom's the year before, but now they were coming to our turf and they would get to follow our rules. No grace before meals, no mini marshmallows on the yams, and Greg and I would not pretend that we slept in separate rooms for them. How could we anyway, since it was a one-bedroom apartment?

What did I care what they thought of me? Why should I care if we had different morals? For them it was immoral to have sex before marriage, immoral to live together, immoral to be homosexual. In my family it was immoral to eat pink salad and even immoral to live anywhere but New York. ("Why would you move to *Boston*?" my father had asked me when I told him of our plan to move to Beantown. "New York is the center of the Universe!") My father took to calling Greg "my sin-in-law" with a broad grin on his face. I doubted that Greg's family saw our situation with such light humor.

On Christmas Eve, I surprised both my boyfriend and his family by suggesting that we attend midnight mass at the historic Trinity Church in downtown Boston. I thought it would be fun, with a choir singing and all the lights in the church shining. But I hated it. There was none of the "ho-ho-ho" kind of thing I had expected. It was somber, boring, and the priest was not at all into my kind of Santa Claus, Jingle Bells Christmas.

I felt more comfortable with Greg's mom after spending the better part of a week with her in my home. She was fun to be with, she was excited to see Boston, and she really did not show any signs of disapproval or judgment about our living together. Megan was a different story. I still felt distant from her and was unsure how to connect with her. Part of the problem was that she seemed very separate from her family, not just me. She would not allow herself to connect with Greg or her mom, and there was tension in the air all around her. It was clear to me that the reality of the family situation was still too painful for her to bear. Her father was gone and was never coming back. He had left, abandoned her, taken his own life. She used her religion as a mask, as a way to keep herself out of the real world, like a big wall around her. I knew after the week we spent together that a connection between us would be hard to come by. Also, in the back of my head, I had the old feeling of fear and insecurity because I was nothing. She was something and I was nothing.

Although each of my parents came to visit after Greg's mom and sister had spent the holidays with us, Greg and I were largely without family in Boston. It was nice that my parents' oldest friends, the Manns, lived in Boston and I could have them as a surrogate family while I was there.

When both couples were newlyweds in New York, my parents had lived in the front apartment and the Manns had moved into the back apartment. They became friends (after borrowing a cup of sugar), and the families (each had two kids, I was the oldest and the only one out of college) were still friends. I adored the Mann family. The kids were smart and funny, and the parents were supportive and warm. They had a big house near my apartment, and I liked stopping by for a dose of family life once in a while.

As Passover neared that spring, the Manns called me to invite me to their seder, and I was delighted to be included in a family holiday. I knew that the seder is held on the first night of Passover, which lasts seven nights. I also knew, partly from the seder of my youth and partly from watching *The Ten Commandments*, that it took the Jews that long to get out of Egypt, to cross the Red Sea that Moses parted (and then closed on the charging Egyptian army), and get to what is now called Israel. I liked the idea of a meal that all Jews had on the same night and that it was as much about a family tradition and a celebration of shared history as it was a religious ceremony.

I hoped that the Manns would not be too into the "God Almighty" stuff. I knew that there was some of that included in the seder prayers and recitations, but I thought that the Mann family would play it down. Greg could not come because he had to be at work (selling those suits). I had not been to a *real* seder since my childhood, where I was the only child at the table, except for the one year my mother had tried to force us all into a tradition we did not have when my grandmother was sick. So I was curious to see what it was all about now that I was an adult.

I arrived right after work, having been instructed to be there by sundown, and after we had drinks we were called to the table to begin. I had a momentary panic as I realized that we were really going to do the whole seder. I had forgotten how formal it was. The table was set with china and crystal, and as we sat we all opened the books to the first page of the prayer book. I opened my copy of the Haggadah, the prayer book that accompanies the seder, from the front, but that was the final prayer of the evening. I had forgotten that the English translation of the Hebrew is read from right to left. I quickly turned my book around and followed along.

It was a very cold night. There was still a bit of snow on the ground, but I had chills from the words more than from the temperature. I enjoyed the readings from the Haggadah, which tell the story of the Jews' plight in ancient times and the perseverance of the Jews through thousands of years of strife, which reaffirms the connection that all Jews have to each other and to the deep traditions of the people. The celebration of Passover invites commentary and discussion. The Haggadah is meant to get the reader to think. That seemed so different from what I knew of some of the Christian ways, where the Bible was not to be questioned. At the Manns' table there was lots of discussion and even disagreement, especially since there were atheists present. Not only was I a nothing, but Mr. Mann's mother, the elderly grandmother at the table, was also irreligious and somewhat impatient with the more reverent passages in the Haggadah. In the end, we all laughed and had fun as we read through the Haggadah, and even though it was meant to reaffirm the Jewish connection to God, with many of the prayers ending with "God is great" or "Praise God," it ended up being more about togetherness than religion.

Then it was time to eat. The food was delicious, as the Manns were excellent cooks. We ended the meal with the statement "Next year in Jerusalem! Next year may all people be free!" The meal ends that way so that the people at the table remember that the Jews were not always free, not in the ancient times and not in the early part of the twentieth century either. It is also a reminder that all over the world, not all people are free, even at that very moment there are many in the world who do not have freedom. As for the Jerusalem part, all Jews are supposed to want to go to that city for seder, as if it's some sort of pilgrimage. I had no interest in going there, but still, the statement gave me a lump in my throat as I felt the importance of the holiday. It was a celebration of spring and the dawn of hope newly born each year, hope that next year would be a better year, not just for me, but for the world.

Sitting there that night, I had a wonderful feeling of tradition and connection with so many other people. So many other people sitting at their seder tables on the same night all around the world for so many generations. I felt a part of something that was bigger than me, bigger than my one life. For that one evening, I felt part of a real history. A history of a people whose religion made them what they are, and even though I never thought of myself as a religious Jew, I did feel Jewish at that moment.

The only problem was that I didn't like all the God references. I didn't really think that God had done, or continued to do, any of the things the Haggadah said he did. Still, I went home that night excited to feel a connection to a religion, even as I rejected the basis for the belief system by not buying into the idea of God as the ruler of all. I was happy to have understood something about this ritual dinner that I had never understood before. I was glad to see that I could participate in something religious without feeling like an outsider or an interloper. When I had been a teenager and my mother had tried to do a seder (that night at my dying Nan's house), I had bristled and refused to participate. But now I saw that it wasn't only about God; it could be about spring-time, new beginnings, freedom, and tradition.

After a year in Boston, I wanted more time to paint, so I moved back to New York. It was difficult to be away from Greg, but we needed time to do our own things. I moved into my old room at Mom's (to save money on rent) and spent a lot of time painting. I got work done, but I began to under-stand the difficulties of unstructured time. Days would slip away, and it was hard to keep the energy going in the studio. I was still using figures in my paintings, but I had also begun to paint my old dolls. I posed them to look cast-off, almost dead, and I wanted the paintings to have an emotional impact. I wanted them to have a story and a message. But I felt that the story I was telling was not really my story, and I was increasingly frustrated with my work.

In the winter, I started to work part-time for an architect who was going to write a book about handmade furniture. I was hired as her research assistant and before long, I was the photography stylist, the chauffer, the caterer, and the travel agent. I liked my job. I had lots of flexibility, so I was still working in my studio when I could.

Greg moved to New York in May. He was sick of under-cover work and digging through garbage, and he had an offer for a job as an entry-level editor at an interior design magazine. He stayed with me at my mother's house while he looked for his own apartment. He could not find any decent apartments that he could afford, but he did find a nice sublet apartment on West 23rd Street, though it was only affordable if I moved in with him. So I did. Even though I had thought it would be a good idea to be in the same city but not be playing house, I was getting sick of living with my mother, and moving in together seemed like the best option for us.

We painted the sublet and were settled in by mid-June. As soon as the paint dried, the troubles started. We didn't really fight, we just didn't want to do the same things. And then we seemed to stop talking. By the middle of the summer, I was sleeping on the couch in the living room instead of in the bedroom with Greg. I pretended it was because it was too hot in the non-air-conditioned room, but really it was just easier. It seemed to me that we wanted such different things; he seemed happy to be settled in New York with a job and an apartment, and he seemed headed for boring stability. I wanted to travel, maybe even go around the world, maybe become a photographer or go to art school somewhere far away and exotic. How could we stay together if I was going to leave him in the dust with all my plans and aspirations?

It had not occurred to me that Greg had already done something I had not yet accomplished. He had left home. I had only just moved out of my mother's house and I lived only ten blocks from her. I still checked in with both my parents at every decision and every event in my life.

As the summer ended, I felt conflicted about Greg and uncertain of our future. We had made plans for a late September trip to California so that we could go to his sister's wedding. As the time drew nearer, I was not very interested in going, but since I had arranged a whole business trip around the weekend in Salinas, I was stuck with the plan. It wouldn't be so bad, the weather would be nice, and the time away from the problems Greg and I were having might give me some perspective on the situation. I didn't feel ready to cut him loose, but I was not feeling connected to him. Somehow I hoped that spending time in his dinky hometown with his conservative, whispering family might bring us back together.

chapter 15

joined in jesus

I picked Greg up at the San Francisco airport on my way south from the photo shoots of houses with art furniture I had set up in Oakland. It was good to see Greg after the days away. The two hours in the car gave us a chance to catch up and prepare for the world that we were about to enter. We knew that the weekend would be intense, since Greg's entire extended family would be there. The wedding was going to be held at the church that Greg had attended as a child, so he warned me that it was going to be a real Christian ceremony. I had never been to a wedding like that. The one church wedding I had been to earlier in the summer had been in a Catholic church, but the acoustics were so bad that I did not hear much of anything that was said at the altar.

As soon as we got to Arlene's house, we started running errands. There was a lot to do; flowers and cakes to be picked up, place cards and programs to be dropped off, and friends staying all over town who needed rides here and there. I remember the stunning September weather—hot but not too hot—and the drives I took all around Salinas and Monterey, which provided needed breaks from the family, the questions, and the constant idle chatting.

The morning of the wedding was a busy one at Arlene's house. The whole family was there; plus the groom and his family were getting ready to get to the church. Jed's brothers, Josh and James, were pleasant enough, and his sister, Joanne, was also nice. She seemed normal, a not-too-Christian kind of normal. It was true that the whole family had names that began with the same letter (except for his mother, Rene), but while I had feared that they were a family of fire-and-brimstone born-agains, they really were not. They seemed to be a normal, churchgoing American family.

After the crowds had left, I was sitting in the dining room with Joanne, having a cup of coffee before I had to get ready to go. Megan was in the back of the house getting dressed to go to the church (where she would get into her gown and veil). She stuck her head in the dining room and beckoned to me and Joanne. We put down our coffee cups and followed her into the bathroom. She had her robe on and she looked worried. The robe fell open and we saw that she was wearing a matching bra and panties set (probably given to her at a shower I had not been invited to). It was white and silky.

"Do I look okay?" she wanted to know. "Does this look, you know, right for tonight?"

Joanne and I both said yes, that she looked great. Joanne said that the matching underwear set was perfect for the day and night ahead. As we returned to our coffee in the dining room, Joanne said under her breath, "Poor Megan. My brother is hung like a horse, and I can't imagine what tonight is going to be like for that girl!" And she winked at me. "You know this is their first time."

As horrified as I was to have this information, I couldn't

help wondering about the stress and pressure that the "first time" must add to an already big event. I thought about the logistics of the honeymoon for two people who had never had sex before: Would they fumble around awkwardly or just know what to do? They had known each other for years, so had they discussed the proceedings? Did they have a plan? I thought about how I had wanted to get the "first time" over with and had not needed it to be special or meaningful. I couldn't really believe that they had been "dating" for over four years and had done little more than kiss.

At the ceremony, I sat off to the side with the old folks from Greg's family, since Greg was a groomsman and was ushering people to their seats before standing at the altar. I had not been invited to be a bridesmaid, I guess because my sinful status was not desirable in the wedding party. That was fine with me, since the girls all had to wear yellow dresses with ruffles and bows. I would have looked dreadful in the getup. The church was dark and oaken inside, with stained glass windows and a big organ. For the special event there were large baskets of flowers and yellow ribbons festooning the place. I sat in the pew and listened to the sermon given as the bride in her flowing white gown and the groom in his rented polyester tuxedo with yellow cummerbund stood stiffly before the minister. I started out with a smile on my face, a pleasant, isn't-this-nice kind of a smile. As the minister went on and on with the "Jesus brought these two together" statements and "the love of Jesus has made this relationship" pronouncements, I started to feel my smile get more and more forced. I had never heard such absurd assertions—that the couple had little to do with where they were in life, that it was all divine intervention that made the relationship. I clenched my fists as he kept talking about Jesus, the love of Jesus, Jesus in the hearts of the betrothed, and Jesus this and Jesus that. My hands hurt because my nails were cutting into my palms. I was incensed thinking about the months of struggle that Greg and I had been through. Months when I had been confused, worried, and spent countless nights wide awake on the couch, not sure what to do. We were working through it, just the two of us, the two people *in* the relationship. Not God, not Jesus, just Greg and I. At that moment I felt how hard relationships were, I felt it right to my core. I realized that it was *work*, a relationship was work that two people had to do. So the sermon that the minister was delivering was not sitting well with my freshly formed ideas. I clenched my fists tighter.

Finally the vows were taken, although by this time, the pain in my palms was distracting and the ceremony was over. The bride and groom walked down the aisle and out into the early afternoon sun. There was rice thrown at them, and then they went to the gym next to the church for the receiving line. The whole congregation was there, and everyone had to have a moment with the newly married couple; plus all the friends and family wanted kisses and hugs. It took hours. I ran around with Greg's little cousins and talked to the grandparents during the time it took to get through the line. Then it was time for cake! Not everyone who had attended the ceremony was coming to the reception, so the bride and groom cut the cake and fed it to each other in the middle of the church gym. I had been in my wedding clothes for hours by this time. My feet hurt, I was tired of smiling at strangers and making small talk as "the brother's girlfriend," and I still had the entire reception to go.

The reception was in Monterey, so Greg and I could vent and laugh in the car before we went back into the "other" world. The reception was downstairs in a nice old building, but it was an institutional-looking room, with gray linoleum tile floors and mirrors along one wall. The yellow color theme did nothing to soften the fluorescent lights, and the music was blaring off the hard surfaces of the room. I scanned the room and quickly realized there was no bar. I knew that the older generation of Greg's family favored their five o'clock cocktails, and I could have used a little something myself at that point, so I was relieved when Greg said that there was a bar down the hall. It was a dark room with some old guys perched on barstools. We ordered rounds of drinks (a dollar a drink) for Greg's family and ourselves and headed back into the hall.

Greg and I delivered the drinks and mingled. I continued to have the same conversation over and over again, and the same conversation countless times with Greg's Uncle Roland whom no one had bothered to tell me was in the middle stages of Alzheimer's. Then it was dinnertime. I was seated at a table with strangers. Greg's family was all seated at the tables up front, and Greg was stuck up on the wedding party platform at the front of the room. I sat down and smiled at all the fellow partygoers around the rectangular table. They smiled back at me, but before we could start to chat, the minister stood and led us all in the blessing. As everyone else bowed their heads and really seemed to be praying, I kept my head down just enough so that I didn't call attention to myself.

I felt very much an outsider by the time the prayer was over. I was the only nonbeliever there, it seemed. I was also the only person at the table who had visited the bar;

everyone else was happy to wait for the champagne toast. For that special moment there were tiny bottles of champagne on each table. Each one was the size of a Coke bottle—the kind that used to come out of vending machines—and was topped with a metal cap. Each person at the table had about a tablespoon of the ol' bubbly in a plastic flute. We were all finishing up our beef stew (which tasted like shoe leather in sauce) when it was time for the toasts. Greg refused to make a toast to his sister, even though I begged and pleaded with him to speak in his father's place. He seemed to be out of place here too. He didn't look like he was having much fun with the rest of the wedding party. I noticed that he was seated next to Lisa, his least favorite of his sister's Christian sorority friends.

After the toasts were over, I sat at the table, waiting until Greg could get off the platform and come with me to get another drink. I was out of things to say to my fellow diners, having already covered the weather, the pennant race, and how we each knew the bride or groom. I was just about to go get that drink alone when the bride and groom arrived at our table for the visit. There were compliments all around on how lovely it all was, what a beautiful dress, touching service, and wonderful reception. I was smiling, nodding in agreement and dishing out the good feelings with the rest of my dinner mates.

By this time, the smile on my face felt painted on and my outsider status seemed to be growing. As Jed and Megan stood there, someone started an "Oh, do you remember . . . ?" story. The people from the table had introduced Jed and Megan many years ago at music school on a double date, Jed and Megan's first date.

"Oh, yes, I remember that night! We went to see that movie."

"Yes, that movie at that place, near that diner."

"That was fun . . ."

"I remember . . ."

I had not had much to add to this moment of memory, but since I was sitting there nodding along anyway, I decided to pipe up with something along the lines of "Cool, you all went out together on the first date? That is really sweet!" I figured I might as well join the conversation, since it was happening right above me.

Jed looked at me with a you-are-a-gnat-buzzing-around-my-head look. Choosing to ignore this, I forged ahead. "What movie did you go see?"

Megan was deep in conversation with someone else at the table by this time, but Jed was standing closer to me. He shook his head at me and answered dismissively, "You wouldn't know it."

"No, really," I said. "I see tons of movies. What was it?"

I was earnestly trying to join in the moment. Jed looked at me with an annoyed expression.

"You wouldn't have seen this one," he insisted.

"Well," I was insistent, too. "Try me." I could not conceive of a movie I had not even heard of. Why wouldn't he just share the title and include me in the conversation? I was being insistent partly out of desperation to connect to someone, anyone. Jed stared at me harshly. "It was called *The Jesus Film*," he mumbled.

"Oh," I gulped. "I guess you're right, I don't know that one." Of course their first date had been a movie with a name like that. Did I expect it would have been *Blue Velvet*?

By this time, Megan was back at our end of the table. She explained that it was a movie about the life of Jesus, based on the Gospel of Luke. The rest of the table nodded and agreed that it had been a great movie, really uplifting, special, and what a great first date!

I turned and saw Greg walking toward the table, having been released from his duty as a member of the wedding party, and removing his yellow cummerbund as a sign of freedom. He motioned with his head to the bar, and we went to fetch the final round for the old folks and ourselves.

I was thoroughly relieved when the reception was over. Megan had changed out of her frilly white dress and was wearing a black-and-white checked jacket and a short black skirt. She and Jed ran through the crowd with more rice and cheering and got into the car (complete with shaving cream and soda cans) to go to a hotel in Carmel for their honeymoon.

We got back to Arlene's house late and exhausted. We sat around the dining room with the groom's family for a while, winding down. The phone rang. It was Megan, calling to tell her mom how beautiful the room was, how they had loved the whole day, and how happy they were. After a few minutes, Jed's sister, Joanne, yelled, "They are just stalling! Hang up! Make them get to it!"

The image of the two of them on their first night, fumbling through what must have been a long-anticipated act, caused me to shudder. I fell asleep trying not to think of them. I did not sleep very well, anyway. The room was cold, and I was thinking about my boyfriend, who was asleep down the hall. Greg had come from this and yet he was so unlike the rest of his family. I admired him for getting out, for refusing to come back, for not living by their rules, and for not making apologies. I finally fell asleep and woke up the next morning with the feeling that Greg and I were not over, that we would not go back to New York and break up. Greg was his own person. It was not that his family was bad; they were actually growing on me. But Greg had really broken away from them; he was so independent. I thought maybe someday I could be like that, too.

chapter 16
tarot cards and taco pie

Greg and I went to Cape Cod not long after we returned from California. We borrowed my mom's new Honda and drove through Newport and out onto the Cape. We stayed in Brewster, about halfway out on the arm of Cape Cod, in an old inn. We spent our days driving around and going to the beach—something I love to do in the crisp, fall days, with bright sunshine warming one side of you and a brisk wind cooling the other. We ate lunch in little diners or we had picnics. In the evenings, after we would go out for dinner, we would return to the quiet inn, where there were few guests in October and no TV. So we listened to the radio, played cards, and got to know each other again. By the end of the week, we were reconnected and we realized that we still liked each other.

During the spring and summer before the trip to Cape Cod, I had dozens of future plans. Some were grand, like traveling, and some were practical, like going to graduate school. But they changed with the weather. By the time the furniture book project was ending and I had to decide what to do next, I was thoroughly confused. To make it worse, my family was getting sick of my crazy ideas. I often had dinner at my father's house and, one night in the early winter, I was there talking about my latest plans for the new year. We were eating pasta with a light tomato sauce followed by chicken piccata. He liked to eat in two courses, a *primo piatto* and a *secondo piatto*, like in Italy. By the time he served the chicken, he was losing his temper with me.

He told me I had no direction, that I was wasting my time, that I was straddling a job and art. I was neither working toward promotions and raises nor was I pursuing my painting to see if I could make a go of that. I cried into my dinner. He pushed me on my options. I told him that I had applied to the New York Studio School and had been accepted to start in January.

The Studio School was on 8th Street in an old brownstone that had once belonged to Gertrude Vanderbilt Whitney. It had been the first location of the Whitney Museum and was now home to the art school, which emphasized working from life. The schedule was simple: You took drawing classes for four hours a day and either painting or sculpture for the other four hours. There was an hour for lunch during which there was usually an artist's talk or an art history lecture. Basically it was total-immersion art school. I was frightened of the leap it required me to take. I could not attend part-time and still have a job. I had to go full-time and really commit.

Dad offered to pay for a semester at the school. He said if I was going to do it, I had to really do it and not be distracted by working at the same time. If I decided to do it, he agreed to write me a check for tuition and three months' rent, but I really had to be sure I was ready. I dried my eyes and decided to go, but I was not ready to take the check. I still had to talk to Greg and give it some thought. I was sure that I would be coming back to get that check, though. I was positive that full-time art school was the right thing. Wasn't it?

Shortly after that dinner with Dad, I spent a lunch hour with a woman from my part-time job who read tarot cards. I didn't think the cards would tell my future, but I really liked Lori. She was funny and sharp-witted and not quite sure what she wanted to do next, just like me. Since my future seemed hazy to me, I welcomed any insight I was offered. I had never given much weight to anything like reading cards, palms, or tea leaves, but I thought it would be fun to see what I could get the cards to "say." Since they all had pictures on them, I was sure it would be easy to play with the images and do some free association with what I saw, like the inkblots I had learned about in an introductory psychology class in my freshman year of college. I picked the number of cards she told me to pick, and we laid them on the desk in some kind of special order.

Lori took it all very seriously, and I did not want to offend her by being irreverent. So I went along with the ritual, knowing that there was no threat of conversion at the end. I would get to see what Lori thought I should do, since she would be "reading" the cards. But I would also get to see what I thought I should do, too, since I would be telling her which ones to read. If there was something in the cards that led her to say I should be a doctor, I would just say, no, not quite right, and she would try to "read" the card differently. So when she finally told me that I was very creative and I should follow that creative energy, I was surprised and shouted, "Yes! That is what I want to do!"

By the end of the lunch, Lori and I had spoken about

many issues in my life, which meant I got to talk about myself for the whole hour. And I ended up with two clear notions from the "reading," one, that I should stay with Greg, the other, that I should go to art school.

The card that "told" me to stay with Greg had an image of a man lying face down with spears in his back. I looked at that card and knew that it was not Greg but rather it was anyone who seemed better than what I had. When I saw that guy lying facedown on that card, I knew that any other man was dead to me. I smiled as I thought, "Greg lives!"

The last card we turned over was the future card, and mine was the magician card. Of course, the magician card made no sense until I gave it some meaning, and I thought of an artist as a kind of magician, someone who could make things appear, like a drawing on paper. So I took that to be an indication I was ready to commit to art school.

The tarot reading had been fun, but I didn't want to become a "tarotist" or whatever people who follow the tarot are called. I had been curious about it and had quenched that curiosity after the one reading. It seemed pretty silly to me that anyone would think that the cards themselves had real powers. However, I left work that day exhilarated, as though I were on the verge of a whole new direction.

Still giddy from the card reading, I suddenly remembered I was to have dinner at Greg's sister's house that evening, at their new apartment. I had not seen them since the wedding and had never been to their home. They had not lived together before the wedding, so they first set up house together when they returned from California. They lived all the way uptown on 123rd Street. I was done with work early, so I went to Times Square to meet Greg at his office.

We went uptown on the subway together. On the way, I told him all about the tarot card reading. I was really excited. I was ready to grasp this new direction with both hands. Greg looked grim as the enthusiasm bounded out of me. He swallowed and looked right at me with a stern expression.

"What the hell is up with you?" I asked, smiling because I was in a good mood and not willing to be brought down.

"Well," he said. "I just have to strongly caution you against telling Jed and Megan about this."

"About what?" I couldn't figure out what was so serious.

"About the tarot cards. For God's sake, Nica, they won't like it. They will think it is evil, mumbo-jumbo, devil stuff."

I laughed. "No way," I said. "No way will they be so ridiculous. It's only a way of looking into what is already there inside of you. I read my cards a certain way because of who I am. I totally led Lori. It's like reading inkblots or analyzing dreams; it all comes from you. The cards are just a way to get you talking, to get you to open up, and they encourage you to make associations with the pictures. Come on, Greg, they aren't really going to say that these stupid cards are evil, are they?"

"They are," said Greg. "Weren't you at their wedding? If I were you, I wouldn't even mention it."

Well, that was like a challenge to me. Of course I had to mention it now.

The apartment Megan and Jed had was New York gold: rent-controlled. That meant as cheap as you can get in Manhattan. They paid a minuscule amount of money for the small studio. We arrived with a six-pack we had picked up along the way and a bit of a sense of dread at being there. We were happy enough to have been invited for dinner, but

I knew we would have to say grace at the table. Greg knew I was going to mention the damn tarot cards, so we were unsure about how the evening would end. He could tell I had decided to bring them up, since he had known me long enough to know when I saw a challenge. He also knew that I was not just being a jerk but rather that I was truly optimistic. I still thought that his sister and her husband would like me and accept me, tarot cards and no religion and all.

After showing us around ("Here is the livingroom-diningroom-bedroom and over here is the kitchen!"), we sat down to dinner. We sat at the oak dining table, a wedding gift that was meant for a spacious suburban dining room but was wedged into a corner so that once you sat you could not push your chair out to get up. When we were all pinned into our seats, Megan took a large casserole dish out of the oven. It smelled pretty good, like something vaguely Mexican. As she set it down, Megan announced that it was taco pie. Upon inspection, I saw there were Fritos on top of it; some were crushed to make a crispy topping, and whole ones were sprinkled around for decoration.

Now, unlike people from the rest of the country, I did not grow up eating any type of casserole. We never owned a Crock-Pot. My parents never preset the oven to cook at a certain time with the food inside it all day. I had never eaten tuna casserole, not even if it had potato chips on top. (Is crushed snack food a requirement for casserole cooking?) The first and last time I ever ate canned tuna was when I was eight, when my father forced me to eat a quarter of a sandwich, and I threw it back up right there at the table.

I had been introduced to more casserole cooking in the three years I had known Greg than in all the years before I met him. His mother even served breakfast casserole. It was the morning after Megan's wedding, and everyone came over for a final gathering before setting off. On the table there were baking dishes of orange goo. It was bread, soaked in egg, layered with bacon, and topped with American cheese. Arlene could not believe I had never had that dish before, and she gave me an extra-big helping of it. And later, the recipe.

After Jed said the blessing (I assumed my usual pose for this, head down so I didn't offend the hosts but eyes open), we started to eat the taco pie. It wasn't so bad, really. It tasted something like the chili we used to eat on family camping trips that came out of a little foil packet. And it had lots of cheese, plus the crunch of the Fritos. Well, it wasn't unpleasant. Megan laughed nervously as she served it. She knew it was a really "American" dish and even admitted getting the recipe from her mother.

Soon enough the small talk offered up a pause, a break in the flow of "How is work?" and "When did you last talk to Mom?" And of course, I mentioned the tarot cards. (How could I not? How could I help myself?)

"I may go back to art school," is what I said. "I'm still not sure yet, it would be quite a commitment to go full-time, but you can only go full-time to the school I want to attend. I am close to being sure. Anyway, my tarot cards sent me positive messages about it just today." My technique here was to prattle on a bit and then slip it in, smoothly and normally.

It didn't work. Or it did, depending on which outcome I had really hoped for. "Tarot cards!" Jed exclaimed as his fork clattered to his plate.

Megan sucked in her breath, shook her head in dismay, and looked right at Jed, waiting for him to smite the evil that had been brought to their table.

"You had your tarot cards read?" Jed demanded an answer.

"Yes," I said, waving my hand as if to say, no big deal. "There is a woman in my office who was offering to read them for anyone, because she is still learning and she likes the practice, so anyway I thought it would be good for me, you know, to see whether I should go to art school and other stuff, like . . ."

Jed cleared his throat to interrupt me. Suddenly there was a zap of tension in the room.

"Tarot cards are the hand of the devil," he said, once I had stopped chattering.

"Well," I said. "I don't know about that. They are very old, steeped in all sorts of strange traditions and histories. They seem kind of interesting."

"They are the hand of the devil," he said again, more gravely and more seriously than before. "They are black magic. They reject the power of God and his son, Jesus. You should stay away from that. You should be careful."

And he picked up his fork and picked at his food a minute before taking another bite. I glanced at Greg, my eyes wide and my expression one of playful shock. He avoided my eyes, because he was on the verge of laughter himself. That would have been a terrible reaction to what Jed saw as a serious moral infraction.

"Okay," I said, swallowing hard. "I'll be careful." And I changed the subject quickly by asking Megan about some dishware pattern or vase on the shelf: "Who gave you that?"

or "Did you get things off your registry?" and that kind of thing. I avoided anything but the most basic pleasantries until it was time to leave.

As soon as we cleared the block, Greg burst out at me, "What did you do?" But he was smiling. He had enjoyed my little cat-and-mouse game. He had been right, of course. He had spent a lot more time around Christians than I had.

I was laughing too, but I felt bad at the same time. In a way, the cat-and-mouse game had been fun, but only because it filled the emotional hole created by what was, at its core, rejection of me as a person. One would think I might have learned my lesson by this time. These people were different from me and seemed to be clinging to the differences. I got the feeling that Jed and Megan wanted to change me, wanted me to believe as they did. I thought back to the Bible ski camp and the ridiculous attempt to baptize me. Hadn't those people wanted to change me by changing my beliefs? Was that what Jed and Megan would try to do? I got the feeling that I had to respect them for their religion, but they were not going to return the favor. They saw me as faithless, dabbling in dangerous black magic, and why would they have to respect that? Accepting Christ as my personal savior was not in my cards. I knew that my beliefs were not well defined, but I felt sure that things would get clearer as I went along.

chapter 17

a civil ceremony

I started art school the following January. Every morning I painted in the enormous studio on the top floor. Every afternoon I drew from the model in the drawing studio in the back of the school. By evening I was exhausted and dirty. I was becoming immersed in the school, not just because of the long hours but also because of the ideas that started to dominate my life. Art at the Studio School was almost like a religion. There was a right way and a wrong way. There was moral art and there was immoral art. There were the gods who were artists that had achieved mythical status; there were saints who were the teachers who had known the gods and taught us their ways; and there were devils who were artists that had sold out or who did not uphold the sacred ideas of paint, the picture plane, and expressionism. For the rest of the winter months I seemed to eat, sleep, and breathe the school.

February came, and Greg wanted to go out for a Valentine's Day dinner. We had never done such a thing before, and I was confused at his insistence that we go out. At first I was vague, mumbling that I might have a lecture or a student opening that night. But he pressed me for the "date." That morning he reminded me three times. I left the house thinking, "Jeeze, what's with him? It's just stupid Valentine's Day."

I arrived at the appointed Italian restaurant on time. I was dressed decently, which at the time was a rarity. I usually looked like an art student, with dirty old clothes, messy hair, and often with charcoal and paint smudges on my face and arms (and legs when it got warm and I wore shorts). We art students were a messy bunch and we wore our messes like badges of honor. I had even washed my face and put on some lipstick before I left school that evening. I was totally surprised when Greg pulled out a little box between the pasta and the main course. By the time we had finished dinner, we were engaged and had a plan for how and when we wanted to get married.

That March, my mother was diagnosed with breast cancer, and at the end of the month, she went to the hospital for a mastectomy. I was calm and cool through the whole ordeal; I had even been with her for the biopsy and had checked her into the hospital the night before the surgery. But when I had to tell my drawing teacher that I would miss his class because I had to get to the hospital to see my mother in the recovery room, I broke down. I sobbed the whole way in the taxi, terrified that my mother would end up sick and die just as my grandmother had. At least Mom was in a different hospital from the one that Nan had died in; I never wanted to go *there* again.

Mom recovered well and was back at work while starting chemotherapy within a few weeks. Greg and I were her support system that spring. We got her to and from the hospital for her chemotherapy and often went with her to her country house in Hillsdale, New York, after her treatments. Once we were there, we would cook whatever she could hold down and encourage her to get rest before we drove her back to the city on Sunday night.

Greg and I wanted to get married in May. It was soon, but we didn't want a long engagement. During our Valentine's Day dinner we had considered eloping or having a small ceremony at the courthouse with lunch at a restaurant afterward, but in the end, we decided to have a judge come to my mom's house and marry us in front of a small gathering of our friends and relatives. The most important part of the wedding plan was the plane reservations for our honeymoon trip to Italy. Once I secured those, we went ahead with planning the actual wedding.

A few of Mom's friends were concerned about having my wedding in the middle of Mom's cancer treatment, but Mom was not going to let her illness interfere with her life or with mine. We planned the wedding for late in May and hoped that Mom would keep all her hair and not be too sick that day.

When Greg told his mother that we were engaged, she wanted to know what kind of church we would get married in. When I was ten and had imagined getting married, I always pictured the inside of a church with an aisle and a long white dress. I always thought there would have to be a minister and that he would always end the wedding with "You may kiss the bride." But I had never felt comfortable in a church, and there was no way I could stand before God and be joined with Greg in our love for Jesus. After Greg got his mom warm to the idea of a judge and a civil ceremony,

she was thrilled. Greg's whole family seemed pleased. His
Grandma Lois sent me a brooch as a welcome-to-the-family
gift, and she and Arlene were coming out for the whole week
before the wedding. Greg's sister was extremely excited, as
newly married people are for impending marriages. Plus she
must have figured that we might have a chance of salvation
from the fire of hell if we were finally married. I am sure she
thought it was time for us to stop our sinning with premarital cohabitation and whatever else we were doing.

The wedding plans came together smoothly over the
three months between our Valentine's Day dinner and our
Memorial Day wedding. Mom had a caterer she used often
and liked, so we hired them, set a menu, and that was done.
They recommended a florist, so I picked out a color scheme,
and that was done. I bought the dress off the rack at Lord and
Taylor, and Greg bought a new suit with my dad one afternoon, and that was done. Gina and Deborah (my only sister
and my best friend) were my "best women"; Greg chose his
best friend from high school and his best friend from college, so our wedding party was done. By mid-April, we had
the place, the judge, the food, the flowers, the clothes, and
the witnesses. Now all I needed was a pair of shoes.

One evening, Greg came back from a dinner with his
sister and he told me that his sister and her husband prayed
for us. He said that she told him this, as if it were a normal,
regular thing that a sister would tell her brother. "We pray
for you guys," I could hear her say, with a far-off, happy
look on her face. And then maybe she said something like,
"And our prayers were answered when you became
engaged!"

I didn't want them to pray for me. They were praying

for my "salvation" and that would require that I become a
Christian, with all that "Take Jesus into your heart" stuff.
They were praying for me to change and that bothered me.
Greg could just laugh at it all, since he wasn't worried that
they might be right. I always seemed to have a little piece
of my brain that cautioned me against being too sure that
there wasn't a God. I figured that it was safe to be an
agnostic. I wasn't saying there was no God, I was simply
saying I wasn't sure. A big question mark in the religion
category suited me just fine, and I resented the fact that
there were soon-to-be members of my family who wanted
to convert me.

Art school ended, and the wedding took all my attention.
By the day before the wedding, the house was set up, the relatives had arrived, Gina and Deborah had their dresses, and
I still needed a pair of shoes. This is no small task when you
have size eleven feet. I went to every shoe store on 8th
Street. There were dozens of shoe stores, with every shoe
you could ever want . . . unless you needed size eleven. Oh,
sure, they had those cross-dressing stiletto heels in sizes up
to eighteen. But if you were looking for a pair of bone-white
pumps, not too high (since I was already an inch taller than
the groom) and not too pointy, forget it. I had visions of
going barefoot, but finally, at one of the last stores on the
street, they had a perfect pair of shoes *and* they had them in
my size. I wept with relief and happiness.

Our wedding was a casual, fun affair. The civil ceremony took about three minutes; it was as short and non-
Godly as could be had. Then we were married and the party
started. We mingled, visited, and laughed. We ate cake,
danced, and threw the bouquet before the night was over.

Deborah caught the bouquet, but she had to wrestle it from Arlene. It turned out that Arlene was the next to get hitched, so I guess since she touched the bouquet first the marriage magic went to her. It was four years before Deborah got married; she had just met David a few weeks before my wedding. But she did end up with him, so that bouquet must have had plenty of romantic magic within the petals of those white roses.

By the end of the evening, I was exhausted and my feet hurt, but I was happy. Greg and I spent our first night as a married couple at the St. Moritz Hotel, on Central Park South. It was marvelous to wake up to breakfast in bed with the entire emerald green park stretching out in front of us. The early morning sunlight was warm and hazy, and we were floating it in, high above the city and far away from anything but that moment. We looked at each other and smiled over our coffee cups. We had done our wedding our way, no church and no God, just a party that was all about our friends and our families, about connecting and reconnecting with people we cared about.

chapter 18

the conversation

The following fall, Greg got a job offer in Washington, DC. I was reluctant to leave my family, our friends, and the Studio School. But there was a graduate program in DC that looked interesting, and after I found out that my favorite teacher would be applying for a teaching job there, I was ready to go. I thought that a fresh start as a married couple in a new city (one that neither of us knew) was exciting and would be a good way for us to get started building a life together.

We found an apartment for less than we were paying in Chelsea with three times the space. We had a real bedroom, with a huge closet, and a dining room. There was a part of the living room that I could use as a studio, at least until I started graduate school in September. I was going to try to paint on my own again, without the teachers to please or a strict schedule to keep.

Leaving the Studio School was hard. I had teachers there who made me feel that if I left the school I would fall from grace and never, *never* be a "real" painter. They were none too shy about telling me that only they held the secrets of what had to be learned in order to be such a painter. I felt as if I were being cast out of the kingdom and therefore I was dead set on proving them wrong.

Meanwhile, in California, Greg's mother went on a blind date. Her friends set her up with a man from the town next to Salinas. He was a retired army officer and a part-time contractor. They went out two times and then got engaged. She had told me, during a long phone call just before we moved, about the first date, about how nice Frank was, how much they had in common, and how she hoped that the second date went as well. So I was shocked and Greg was speechless when she called two weeks later to tell us she was getting married. It wasn't just shock of the news of the marriage after only a few dates: Frank was black. He was light-skinned, Arlene had said, he almost looked white. But Arlene's family was old-fashioned, and she told me her deceased father was "rolling over in his grave." The fact that Arlene was marrying a black man did make the few elders in the family uncomfortable, and I wondered if they had been shocked at me in the same way.

We moved into our DC apartment right around the first of February. We dumped the boxes and caught our plane to California, leaving everything in chaos. It was only for a week, so we knew we would settle in as soon as we got back.

We planned to stay with Arlene. There was much to be done to help with the wedding, plus we wanted to meet Frank a few times before the big day. Our first night there we went out to dinner with the newest bride and groom and with Jed and Megan. Frank seemed nice enough; he had an infectious laugh and seemed very upbeat and positive. He had been in the army for many years and had fought in Korea and Vietnam, but he didn't like to talk much about war. The fact that he was black didn't matter to either of Arlene's children, but it was funny that Greg's mother was marrying an almost perfect stranger . . . who happened to be black.

Jed and Megan had arrived first and claimed the real bedroom, so Greg and I had to sleep on the couch in the TV room. Since we were all married now, we could sleep in rooms with our significant others. Arlene's cute little house on Oak Street had been sold, and Arlene and Frank would be moving into a new, bigger house a few blocks away. The reception was going to be at the new house, which was mostly empty and therefore a great place for the party. They would finally move into the new place after they got back from their honeymoon in Hawaii.

There were no real caterers for the reception, but a friend of Arlene's was providing some food and the church ladies would be bringing salads. I was afraid there would not be enough for everyone to eat. There were more than a hundred people coming for lunch, but all the lunch consisted of was a platter of chicken "drumettes" (chicken nuggets shaped like little drumsticks) and a huge pot of linguini with clam sauce. It didn't look like nearly enough to feed everyone. Plus, as an Italian American, I was appalled at the idea of serving reheated noodles with canned clams. But I held my tongue and helped set up with all the enthusiasm I could muster. I even ironed tiny ribbons to tie onto the bushes outside the new house.

I was busily ironing away while the rest of the family was gathered in the living room of the new house, doing other little chores. There was no furniture other than a few folding chairs and the grandfather clock we had brought over from Oak Street the night before. We were all doing odd jobs to prepare the new house for the party and we were chatting about local gossip.

"You know that Jan Smith has left First Pres?" Arlene asked. By this time I knew that "First Pres" was the name of their church in town, but I did not know who Jan was. That was not unusual, since Arlene was always talking about Salinas people I did not know. She expected Greg to know all of them, which he usually did not. "Apparently she has turned to some kind of new age thing."

Megan gasped, shook her head, and uttered words of dismay. "That is just awful," she said, "just terrible." She looked like she might cry. That is how upsetting the words "left the church" were to her. Jed was likewise shaking his head, even though I assumed he did not know Jan Smith any more than I did.

"What's so bad about that?" I asked. I didn't even give myself time to think about what I was saying. I was so surprised that someone else's choice of belief would be of such concern to other people, I did not even think that by questioning it, I would be opening myself up to the kind of trouble that would last for years.

I sensed that I had misspoken as soon as the words left my mouth. "I mean, isn't the important thing that she is happy?"

It seemed as if Greg and his mother were both holding their breath. They seemed to know what was coming next and they seemed to fear it. I went back to ironing, realizing that I should have kept my mouth shut, but also knowing that I could not. Not when it was a chance to get them to say what I thought they always wanted to say to me. Maybe if they admitted that they had problems with me—with my beliefs— maybe then we could clear it all up and move on.

"That kind of thing is very dangerous," Jed finally said. I immediately thought of the "dangerous tarot cards" and did not look up for fear of catching Greg's eye and laughing at their seriousness. "To stray from the one truth is a bad, evil thing."

"*One truth?*" I asked. "What do you mean by *one truth?* There are as many truths as there are people in the world." I was getting in deeper now, but I had started it and could not turn back.

"No," yelped Jed, "there is only *one* truth. The truth of Jesus Christ is the only truth that is real, redemptive, the one truth that offers salvation and eternal life. 'I am the Truth and the Way and the Light,' Jesus said. 'The only way to the father is through the son,' says the Bible. 'Deliver me from evil for I have sinned, that I may walk with thee in eternity.' Jesus is truth. The one truth."

I stood there, iron raised but unable to move. I set the iron down and looked around the room. Arlene was getting busier now and was unpacking glasses with real intensity. Greg was in the other room; he couldn't stand this kind of conversation, so he had wandered out. Megan was nodding her head in slow agreement with her husband.

"Wait a minute," I said. "How can there be one truth? What about all the other religions in the world? They all have truths, too. What about the Hindus or the Muslims? They go through life believing that they have spirituality, enlightenment, and eternal reward, but they never worship Christ. What about them?"

"Well," Jed continued to be the spokesperson. "They simply don't understand. If they *did* understand, then they would turn to Christ and accept him as the only truth, the only way. He is the son of God. God sent his only son to this earth to die for us, to suffer for our sins so that we may have eternal life, with him."

I snorted and shook my head. It was just like Bible ski camp. They were just as closed-minded and freakish as those born-again Bible-thumpers I had spent that week with back in high school. I shuddered to think that I was back there again, back in that basement being sermonized for three nights, back in that common room being asked to come forward, be baptized, and accept Christ as my personal savior. No. I wouldn't sit silently this time, I wouldn't push up against that back wall and wait until it was over. This attitude was not right. It was intolerant and disrespectful. I couldn't let it lie unchallenged.

I tried and tried to be clear. I rephrased the statement about five times. "How can you say that the millions of non-Christian people are missing the real truth? How can you say that your way is better than anyone else's way? It isn't like there is empirical evidence of who actually gets saved and who gets left behind." But they kept deflecting the logic. They kept up the absolutes and the arrogance. Megan repeated herself many times, saying, "If we could just explain it to you, I am sure you would understand." And I kept answering, "I don't think I want to understand this."

Finally I said, "Let me get this straight. The other people in all the other religions just don't 'understand,' and if they did 'understand,' they would surely see the light and the truth as you have defined it."

"That is right," they said. Megan even smiled a little, hopeful smile, as if maybe I would "get it" and they would win me over to their way of seeing things.

"Does that mean," I asked, "that those who choose to stick with the belief system that is truth *to them* just don't 'understand'? So they are . . ."

"Wrong," Jed said. "They are wrong."

"Hold on, did you say 'wrong'?" I asked. "So does that mean that you think I am wrong if I choose to stick with what I believe in, even though you have tried to get me to 'understand'? If I don't agree with your way, then I am wrong?"

"Yes," Jed said. "You are wrong to reject Jesus. You are wrong to not think he is what we say he is."

I put the iron down. I stared at them. "So," I finally said, "I am supposed to respect you and your beliefs, but you cannot do the same for me?"

"That is right," they both said, almost at the same time. As I turned and walked away, one of them said, "We cannot respect you if you reject Christ." I don't even remember who said it, but it didn't matter by then.

I opened the front door and went outside to the porch of the new house. It smelled strongly of cat piss, but I had to get out of that room. I sat on the step and stared at the street. What had just happened? How did I get from ironing tiny ribbons to being told I was wrong? I had always hated being told I was wrong, since my parents told me that all the time.

I was furious. Partly because they told me I was wrong, but also because I really did want them to accept me for who I was, even if I was nothing. I didn't want them to want to change me. I didn't want their prayers or this lecture and I didn't want to be wrong. I could see that there was an ultimatum on the table: accept Christ and we will accept you, otherwise, well, you're just plain wrong.

I sat there thinking, "Wrong, wrong, I am wrong," and somewhere deep inside I was worried. "What if I am wrong? What if there is a God and a hell and I end up there writhing with pain in the fires for eternity?" Well, even though I had my worries, I couldn't believe they had actually said that I was wrong to be who I am. Greg came out and sat down with me. He shook his head.

"Assholes," he muttered. "Mom is way pissed at them. She has enough to worry about without this family drama."

"Well," I laughed, "at least I know where I stand now. At least they said it, you know. After the 'we pray for you' thing, and the 'tarot cards are evil' thing, I guess they have finally made their feelings clear to me."

I mostly stayed away from Megan and Jed for the rest of the weekend. If, during the wedding party, I found myself near them and unable to avoid them, I would scan the room for a quick escape, like an uncle who needed a fresh drink or a pile of paper plates to throw away. I threw myself into helping at the reception. The room was full of churchgoing Christians, and I wondered if they all thought I was "wrong." Maybe I could have quieted them all down with a *clink-clink* on a wine glass and we could have taken a vote.

I tried to be more helpful, smile a bigger smile, and be more interested in the guests than Jed and Megan were. I was going to show them who was right, and if I couldn't be right, at least I could be better.

chapter 19

open casket

those first months in DC were tough. I knew no one, Greg worked long hours at his new job, and I was spending most days alone. I went to the National Gallery every week and painted in my studio at home for many long, solitary days that spring. I did get into the graduate painting program at the American University with a full scholarship, and Stanley, my favorite teacher, did get the job. He was from the Studio School and had been a wonderful and supportive voice there. I was glad he would be teaching me again, since he was considered a "real" painter. With him at my side, I knew I would soldier on in my quest for authentic painting.

By April, Greg and I had made new friends and we were getting into the groove of the nation's capital. Greg and I even had our first "couple" friends: they were introduced as a "they" and we as a "we." I started graduate school in September and found myself busy with my own classes, plus teaching undergrads as part of my scholarship, painting in the studio on campus, and socializing with friends at school.

I liked school, was learning every day, and was feeling less aligned with the Studio School way of thinking about art. It was good to be around students who were not part of

that philosophy. I came to realize that there is no single way
to be a "true" painter. I enjoyed the experimentation and
variation in my studio. The philosophy of the Studio School
was beginning to feel too much like the narrow-minded and
limiting philosophy of my in-laws.

The first year of graduate school was the year my Italian
grandmother was dying. Grandma Emily, my father's
mother, was a tiny old woman from my earliest memory of
her. By the time she died, she was in her nineties, although
no one seemed sure exactly how old she really was.
Grandma had lived in the Bronx since she got off the boat
from Italy. She never went anywhere again, other than to
Westchester to visit her daughter and to Manhattan, once, for
a Christmas dinner at our house. I didn't ever feel that I
knew her very well. She was not like Nan to me; I never
slept over at Grandma Emily's or went to the movies with
her. She didn't go to movies. She had worked her whole life
as a wife, a mother, and a seamstress. By the time I saw her
regularly, once we had moved to New York and had holiday
gatherings and Sunday afternoon visits with her, she still
cooked and sewed (even with her bad eyesight). But she had
always seemed old, and her thick Italian accent made it hard
for me to understand her. Mostly she fought with her sister,
Great-aunt Lucy, who lived upstairs.

Lucy and Emily used to fight as if they were still children. They would argue, bicker, bait, and tease. Sometimes
it was mean-spirited, but most of the time it was just plain
ridiculous. They were both widows and they would even
argue about their dead husbands. My Grandfather Lalli had
died when I was eight or nine. I had refused to visit his grave
when we visited New York the Christmas after his death. I

simply would not get into the car. My mother was apoplectic with rage at my refusal, but my Aunt Jean interceded and calmed her down. Jean never made her kids do anything—they didn't even have to clear their dishes after dinner—so a kid not wanting to go to the cemetery was no big deal to Jean. I still remember my mother glaring at me as I waved to her and the rest of the family getting into the cars to go to the graveyard.

It turns out that my grandfather was not such a nice guy. He was once described to me (when I was an adult) as "a wife beater" with a generally bad disposition. I had always liked him, with his funny old hats, his old-fashioned suits, and his Black Jack gum. I actually hated the taste of Black Jack gum (it was licorice flavor), but I loved getting it from him. I loved the way he took it out of his pocket, like it was a big surprise, and made such a grand gesture as he handed it out, only one piece per grandchild.

By the time my grandmother died, she had been in a nursing home for a few months. The last time I saw her alive was the summer before she died. My dad and I rented a car and drove to Our Lady of Mercy Convalescent Hospital in the Bronx to see her. It was a dingy place, with ugly colors on the walls and a smell of urine and stale cooking that hung in the halls. But the nuns who ran the place were pleasant, and Grandma seemed to be getting good care. She did not recognize me or my father when we came into the room. She looked at us with confusion and a bit of fear in her eyes. Then she snapped into our reality and knew who we were, only to drift back away. At one point she sat up a little and raised one hand up, pointing to the ceiling with trembling fingers.

"What?" my dad asked. "What is it, Ma?"

She dropped her hand and looked at him, startled that anyone else was in the room, then she turned her head away from him, closed her eyes and said, "No."

Dad looked at me and shrugged; he did not seem to know what else to say or do. Aunt Jean and Great-aunt Lucy came while we were there. Jean looked worried as Grandma seemed to slip further away from reality, and Lucy looked mad, like she was upset that her older sister was getting all the attention. At one point, Grandma became quite lucid, and while Lucy was in earshot, Grandma announced that she wished to die.

"That's a sin!" Lucy yelled. "A sin and you'll go to hell for it!"

"Bah," my grandmother waved her frail hand at her sister. "What do you know?"

"It's a sin, that's what I know!" Lucy glowered at her sister. "Don't say it again, I don't want to hear it."

Aunt Jean finally told them both to stop; she told them that they would wake the rest of the patients with their yelling. They obliged, but glared at each other for the rest of the visit.

I got the call from Dad first thing on a Friday morning in November. "Grandma died last night." I got on the next train home to New York. The wake was that night, and the funeral and burial would be on Saturday. As I sat on the train, I wondered why I didn't feel sad. She was old, I rationalized, and it was time. Plus, I had never had a relationship with her away from the family, so by the time I was in high school, the Sunday visits were more of an obligation than a day of fun. We would sit in her cramped kitchen and eat, and sometimes my mother would ask a lot of questions and get Grandma and Lucy to talk about the old country. But that usually ended in a fight, and Aunt Jean would have to change the subject by asking one of us about school.

As I walked into the Ferrara Funeral Parlor with my father, I realized that I had never been inside one of these places before. I met my cousin Bill outside the room that had been set aside for us, for our family. Bill looked pale. He had never been to one of these places either, and there was an open casket in that room. We shook our heads at each other, grimaced, and shrugged. We weren't comfortable about the idea of facing a dead body. I swung the door open and we walked into the room. At one end, there was a big, ornate box with a waxy-looking woman lying in it. There were lights shining on her, and she was wearing a pink, filmy dress. In her hands she held a rosary. Her eyes were closed. Bill and I crept toward her, sort of leaning on each other. When we got close enough to see her clearly we sat in chairs that were lined up in front of the casket. Then we sighed. The worst was over. We were in and we were looking at our dead grandmother, at a real dead body just lying there in the carpeted room with red velvet curtains and flocked wallpaper.

Aunt Lucy arrived as Bill and I were congratulating ourselves on making it into the room. She walked up to the body, knelt on the little bench in front of her sister's coffin, crossed herself, stared hard at Grandma and said, "She looks good. They made her look nice." Then she hesitated and mumbled, "But what did they do to her mouth? It looks a little funny." Then she crossed herself again, looked at us and said, "I hope she gets to heaven, with all that talk of wanting to die, you never know."

Hours later, as the wake was ending and people were saying their good-byes, Brother Bernard came into the room. He was a large man, tall and broad in his black robes, with white, white hair, piercing blue eyes, and a soft, boyish face. In a booming voice, Brother Bernard said a prayer for "Dear Sister Emily." I was impressed by his entrance, his presence, and his eloquence. When he spoke, I was mesmerized. And he did not think death was sad; he thought of it as a chance to celebrate the life of the person. He made me feel it was fine that I wasn't sad about my grandmother, and he was sure she was in a far better place.

I liked what he was saying, but I felt disconnected from the promises of eternal rewards and the happiness that awaited my grandmother in heaven. I certainly did not think she was being released from this earth. She was lying in that coffin, and then she would be put in the ground. She wasn't going anywhere else after that, I was sure. The only thing that mattered was that she was no longer suffering here; there was no way her suffering all those years on earth would be erased by Jesus in heaven. But I was glad that the other members of my family, especially Aunt Lucy, seemed comforted by what Brother Bernard was saying. I knew that for Lucy, heaven was an important idea. In some ways, I felt that it was the easy way to go, the way to feel less loss around death. It was too bad I didn't have that, but I just didn't.

The next morning, Brother Bernard was with us at the brief service we had at the funeral parlor. He explained to us that he was a brother because he was a missionary, a monk, but not an ordained priest. Later, at the church, there was a real priest, an old man who spoke in a sort of monotone and swung all the incense around and mumbled some incoherent prayers. He did not seem to have known my grandmother, and the rote words of comfort he gave us seemed hollow. I didn't mind being there, since I figured it would have meant something to my grandmother, but I was eager for the church part to be over. It seemed to be simply what was "done" as part of the funereal day, and Lucy seemed happy to be there even though the rest of us were restless and a little bored. The priest offered the Communion to all those present, and none of our family accepted the offer. I thought Lucy would go forward to partake in the weekly ritual, but she declined. Later she told us that she just couldn't go up there; she had sinned too badly in the last week by wishing that she, too, might die.

I was glad to have Brother Bernard back at the graveside. He seemed to have known my grandmother, although my Aunt Jean was not sure they had ever met. And he seemed to understand that Emily was old, she lived too long, and now she was dead. He didn't seem to mind that we were dry-eyed as we stood by the freshly dug grave.

As he read from a little prayer book before we left Grandma Emily to be buried next to my grandfather, a bee buzzed around the flowers that were resting on the top of the casket. Brother Bernard paused in his reading and looked at the bee.

"Bees are a very good sign," he said. "A sign of everlasting life."

After a moment more, he returned to the prayer.

The graveside service ended, and we said good-bye to Brother Bernard. I wanted to hear more about him and his way of life. It seemed like something from the Middle Ages, living in a monastery like that, praying many times a day, and living simply without worldly possessions. But it was time to go. He declined the offers of a ride back to the church, and we left him there.

We decided, since it was just past noon, to go out to lunch on City Island. Dad had always talked about how strange it was, like a little New England whaling village in the middle of the Bronx, and I had never been there. We went to the Lobster Box and asked for a table in the room overlooking the water. We were a strange crowd: my father, his sister, three cousins, and the ex's. My mother and my Uncle Saul joined us, even though my parents had been split for years and my aunt and uncle had been separated for decades.

As we ate our lobster *Fra diavolo* and linguini *alle von-gole*, I thought of Grandma. She had been born in a different century, in a town that was most likely wiped away by an earthquake, in a country she never saw again. She traveled by boat to New York as a teenager and had an arranged marriage to my cruel grandfather. She lived her life cooking, cleaning, working, and raising her children. After she was widowed, she went to church, to the market, she got old, and then she died. Brother Bernard was sure she was a child of God and that God would take care of her for eternity after all the suffering she endured in this life. It hardly seemed fair. Why did she have to suffer so much while on this earth? I tried to take comfort in the fact that there was the possibility of reward in death.

And I thought of the bee, buzzing lazily in the flowers of her death. I wondered if the bee was indeed calling her to the world beyond, offering hope of the sweet hereafter. I wondered if she would get to heaven just because she believed in it. I knew that she was dead and in that dark, scary hole in the ground, next to the old coffin that held her not-so-beloved husband.

I knew that the idea of life after death was not one I could hold onto, not even for the comfort it could bring. I hadn't liked the coffin, the grave, or the whole ritual that we had just gone through. I would be cremated, that was for sure. I could take comfort in that. As for my grandmother, if there was comfort for her in death, I hoped she had found it, whether it was in the finality that I saw in death or the eternity that she saw in it.

chapter 20

doubting god

During my second year of graduate school, while I was working on my final painting projects for my master's degree in fine art, Greg decided to apply to business school. He was not sure what he wanted to do with a business degree, but he was sure that without it, he would be stuck in middle management. If he wanted to rise to the top, in publishing or in any other business, he would need that master of business administration degree.

I finished school in May, ending the year with my final show, which was a big success. I had twenty paintings in the small gallery on campus, ranging from abstract to more figurative paintings of rooms and interior spaces. I now had my utterly useless master's degree. After I spent a month teaching at a summer program for young painters, we packed up and moved north, to Hanover, New Hampshire, so Greg could attend the Tuck School at Dartmouth College. It was quite a shock to leave the warm and friendly southern city of Washington, DC, for the cold and conservative New England town of Hanover. Tuck was known for its strong academics and close-knit community. The school was a great fit for Greg, since he was looking for a solid generalist approach to his studies. The business students and their wives were a nice but conventional bunch of people. The worst things about my two years as a "Tuck Partner" were the long winters (complete with one hundred inches of snow each year) and the fact that I just didn't fit in with the culture. I did not fit in with the other Tuck wives, many of whom had babies or small children and had come to New Hampshire from the suburbs. They dreamed of minivans and larger, more comfortable houses back in the suburbs. They did not swear and they went to church.

I knew I was really in trouble when, in the first month of school, I was invited to a Saturday night movie party. The men were off on some all-night project, and the "girls" had rented *Sister Act* and baked a big batch of peanut butter brownies. They called to see if I would like to come on over and join them. I had already gathered my own supplies for the evening at home: I had rented *Drugstore Cowboy* and had purchased a six-pack of Rolling Rock. But I said I'd come over when my movie was finished. I drank four of the beers as I watched my movie: I had not intended to drink that many, but the movie was so tense, the characters were high for most of the two hours, and I was swept into the drama and conflict. So one after the other, I sucked the beers down. As I turned off the VCR when the movie was over, I thought, "Well, I guess I could use a peanut butter brownie right about now," and I weaved over to Mary Lu's house.

Mary Lu was from Texas. She was a Baptist who had never had so much as a sip of alcohol in her life, not even a champagne toast at her wedding. She was tall and lovely, with long brown locks and a wide smile. I knew that after the bare niceties, she and I would have nothing to say to each other. Mary Lu and the five or six other wives were happy I had come over, smiling as they offered me the plate of sweets and sat me down to ask me what my movie had been about. I was unsure how to describe the drugs, the sex, the stealing, the lying, and the overdose deaths that had been constant in the movie. So I kept the description brief: "Oh, well, it was about these people who are drug addicts and they rip off drugstores and have a kind of adventure. How was *Sister Act?*" All the fresh, smiling faces beaming at me made the four beers seem stronger. They had loved *Sister Act*, and they offered me another brownie as they recounted the funny sight gag of Whoopi Goldberg in a nun's habit. I took the second brownie and quickly made my excuses so I could get back home. I was not asked to join in any more movie nights, and in retrospect, I wondered if it had been the smell of beer on my breath that put them off.

But my life in Hanover wasn't all bad. There were good things, too. I had a studio and painted almost every day. I went there every evening after my day job as a sales clerk at the local art supply store. I was happy to be in my own studio rather than in school trying to please my teachers. I ended up winning a cash award from Vassar for my painting after the first winter in Hanover. I painted even more after that and had a few shows around Hanover and at Vassar. I taught a class at a local junior college, and by the time we left, I had a good direction in my studio.

Actually, I packed up my studio in June, two years after I had arrived, because my baby was due in the beginning of August. I lost two pregnancies before the third one stuck and I was nervous throughout the second trimester. The miscarriages had been awful, painful, and totally unexpected. I thought only older women, sick women, or women with "problems" had that happen to them. My pro-choice views made it difficult for me to think of those six-week-old fetuses as babies. I was sad and devastated by the lost pregnancies and yet I put forth a calm, rational front.

The first one was a total shock. I found out I was pregnant on a Tuesday and I told everyone I saw. I could not think of a reason not to spread the good news. Two weeks later I had to un-tell everyone. Some of my Tuck-wife acquaintances said things like "It was God's will" or "The baby is in God's hands now." But I wasn't even sure that there had been a baby. I was not comforted by the words of reassurance phrased in religious terms. I was angry, disappointed, and confused. But I did not think, as I had earlier in my life, that I was being punished. I was simply a statistic; one in ten first pregnancies ends in miscarriage, often before the twelfth week.

"Oh, yes, well, I was pregnant, but now I'm not," I convinced myself and anyone else who asked. "But six weeks, well, that is hardly a pregnancy. I mean it wasn't like there was really a baby, it was just a blob."

When I spoke to my sister-in-law about the blob, she was direct. "It was a baby," she insisted. "Surely you saw it as a baby, as a life."

I answered that I was sure it was not a baby and that it may or may not have been a life, but it didn't matter now because it was gone. I was not going to let her go any further, so I made an excuse to get off the phone before she got into the God's will stuff. I didn't want to hear it, it just made me angry that people could believe in a God that would make me have a miscarriage and cause me so much suffering.

I told no one, other than family, about the second pregnancy and miscarriage. My mother was sad and shocked. She had not had any miscarriages and so she figured I would never have them, either. She tried to distract me from the loss. She brought me to New York City for the week and took me shopping, out to dinner, and to a show. When I returned, I had no one to share my sadness, no one at Tuck knew about that second blob. I eventually told a few people, the ones who could understand me and wouldn't tell me to put my faith in God. After a few weeks of holding it all in, I broke down and cried for an entire Monday. It was more fear than sadness, though. While I had to admit that I was mourning a loss, I was actually more fearful of never having a baby. The fear vanished two months later when I became pregnant again.

The second winter was as cold as the first, and we had the same one hundred inches of snow. I was sick for most of the winter, from the pregnancy, and I was always tired. But I painted and kept busy and by March, I was feeling good and getting excited that I would really have a baby this time.

We tended to have more visitors once the ground thawed a bit, and that year Jed and Megan came up from New York City for a visit in April. It had been ages since we had seen them, but they could only stay a day or two. Greg had tons of schoolwork while they were there, which left me to entertain them. The first night, we all went to see the movie *Shadowlands*, which was based on the life of C. S. Lewis. I was interested in C. S. Lewis as the author of my favorite children's books, *The Chronicles of Narnia*, and Jed and Megan were interested in C. S. Lewis as a big-time Christian writer. I had always loved the *Narnia* books, even after I found out about all the Christian symbolism in them. For all the times I ran away from anything remotely tied to Christianity, I never did lose my love for those books.

We all liked the movie, which was about the woman C. S. Lewis falls in love with and marries when he is an older man. But then she gets sick and dies of cancer, which throws him into all kinds of doubt about his belief in a benevolent, fatherly God. On the way home from the movie theater that night, we had an interesting discussion about religion. Part of the reason for the discussion might have been that the movie had touched on Lewis's shaken faith after the death of his wife, and Jed also admitted to having had questions of faith. I was surprised that they had ever had a qualm about their rock-solid righteousness and more surprised that they would share that qualm with someone like me.

The next day, before they drove back to New York, they presented me with a book. They had gone to the Dartmouth bookstore and found it for me. I was surprised that they had gotten me a present and thought it was so nice of them. I looked at the title, which read *Doubting God* in large letters.

"Oh," I said, a little unsure of how to take this gift. "Thanks. Thanks so much."

"Jed read this recently and found it so, so helpful. Like we were saying, he had that time when he was in doubt about his own faith. This is such a wonderful book."

"Great, great! I will definitely read it. I am very interested in, um, these kinds of things." And I was a bit interested. I had been thinking about finding a book about religion and had even gone to the bookstore to get one. But once there, I had no idea what to look for and I wasn't even sure what to ask for, so I bought a cookbook instead.

I had always been interested in finding out more about belief systems, but I never seemed to actually find anything out. In college I had considered taking a comparative religion course, but they never offered an introductory level class at a time that fit into my schedule. So even after four years of a well-rounded liberal arts education, I had never taken any religion classes. I also wanted to know more about alternatives to religion, like atheism, but I figured that atheists just were what they were. How could there be books about believing in nothing?

After Megan handed me the book, I looked at the black and purple cover thinking it might be helpful. I looked up at her, then back down again, flipping the book over to read the back cover to stall for time while I figured out what to say. I could tell right away that it was not going to help, since all the blurbs were from people who had reaffirmed their belief in Christ with the help of the author, with his guidance and his love of Christ. I did not need to read this book. I didn't doubt God's redemptive powers; I doubted that he existed at all. I finally smiled and thanked them again. I put the book on the table and followed them outside to say good-bye.

After they left, I asked Greg what to do. I didn't really want to read that book, especially after looking it over. I determined quickly that it did talk about problems the author had with Christianity but that it also led the reader back to a reaffirmation of faith in God and the Bible. The more I flipped through it, the less I wanted to read it. But Greg said I should, it was only polite, after all.

"That is easy for you to say, since you are not the one they gave it to!" I snorted. "Would you read it if you were the recipient?"

"No way!" he answered. "But you should. You are more open-minded. Plus you can tell them you read it and maybe it will help in the long run."

So I read it. Cover to cover. I neither enjoyed it nor learned from it. It was a trick to get into another argument for believing in God. Even though the title suggested it was a fair, cool look at the idea of God, there was nothing fair or cool about this book. The guy who wrote it was just like my in-laws, just as smug and certain about his "way" and his "truth." The "doubting God" part was in the first chapter but was argued away by all the Amens and Hallelujahs that took up the bulk of the pages.

"Now what?" I thought after finishing the last page of newly rediscovered devotion. Although I had hoped that the book might open a dialogue that could help me understand how I could be right without becoming a Christian, it didn't. The author had wrapped it all back around to a strong belief in God, and in the end reaffirmed that to be "right" one must believe in Jesus, which meant I was still "wrong." I determined with Greg that I would give them back the book, even though they had given it to me as a gift. I decided to pretend I thought it was a loan.

We met them for brunch one warm, late spring day in New York. We were in town for my baby shower and Greg's job interviews. Greg was still looking for work, even though he had graduated and many of his classmates had already started with big, fancy companies. Greg didn't want the cut-throat money-jobs his fellow Tuck graduates were hunting down. He wanted a job that was a general management position in a media or publishing company; he was just having bad luck getting an offer. Our baby was due in August, and barring anything else cropping up in another town, we were planning to move to New York in late August and take it from there.

We met Jed and Megan at EJ's Diner on the Upper West Side. They were still living in the rent-controlled studio uptown, so we met them near their building to make it easy for them to get there on time. By the time we got there and got seated, I was starving. I had gained a lot of weight in my pregnancy; I ate what I wanted and it showed. I didn't care; I was feeling well after months of being "morning sick" for eight hours a day, and food was a source of fun. I couldn't drink, it hurt to walk, I was tired all the time, but I could eat with no problem. We had a huge breakfast, my second of the day. We decided to walk downtown for a few blocks to walk off the food, although I waddled more than walked by my eighth month.

We parted ways with the in-laws at the corner of 79th Street and Amsterdam. I wanted to go to the maternity shop, and they had to go to rehearsals. As we said our good-byes, they gave us a little toy for the baby; it was a funny frog toy for the bath, and we all laughed about it. I took the book out of my bag as I was still giggling and handed it back to them.

"Hey," I said, "I finished this and I thought you might need it back."

They seemed a little confused. "No," they said. "We don't need it, but if you don't want it, we'll take it."

"Yeah," I said, "I'm done with it, so go ahead." I held it out and they took it slowly, with uncertainty.

I didn't know what else to say about the stupid book. I hadn't enjoyed it, so I couldn't really tell them that I had. I had already said I read it, so I couldn't really repeat myself to tell them that again. So I said, "Thank you, thank you for loaning it to me."

And they said, "You're welcome, yeah, no problem."

I wonder if they expected me to read that book and *understand*, you know, "See the Light"? Did they really think I would finish the book and run to the nearest church for a full-emersion baptism and a newfound glory in my relationship to God with a personal savior to boot? I don't think they gave that book to me to generate much of a conversation about religion; it presented a pretty one-sided argument for Christianity. In other words, I didn't see a lot of unknowns left at the end of the treatise laid out in *Doubting God*. It was really about *not* Doubting God; it was all about entering a deeper and more meaningful relationship *with* God.

I felt immense relief after handing the book back. Like a sort of exorcism, I no longer had to think about it anymore. I felt good because I had read the book; I had given it the thought and attention it deserved as a gift from a family member and I had given it back as a way of rejecting it. It was a way for me to let them know that my conversion was not imminent.

Greg and I stood for an extra moment on the sunny street corner as Megan and Jed walked away from us, back uptown to get their car. We smiled at each other and squeezed hands. I nodded and said, "Okay, then. That's done." And we went into the maternity store to buy some new clothes for my ever-expanding body.

chapter 21

leap of faith

If there is ever a leap of faith undertaken in this life, it is taken when one decides to become a parent. I learned to have faith that everything would be okay, even after two pregnancies that ended badly. As I neared the end of the nine months of that third "try," I had to build up faith that I could get the baby out of me and that both the baby and I would survive the birth. Then I had to have faith that I would be able to take care of the little creature, that I would know what to do, when, for how long, and how much. I had to have faith that Greg and I would be great parents.

I spent the summer months reading birthing and parenting books in between attending birthing and parenting classes. Greg, the baby, and I would be moving to New York soon after the birth, so I had to pack up our house. I loaded boxes in between lying on the couch with my feet up for hours a day (to try to reduce the swelling that left me unable to wear all but one pair of shoes) and taking walks around the neighborhood to try to get labor to begin. By the time Amelia was born (two weeks late), I was ready to push the baby out of me, ready to be a mom, and ready to start a new chapter of life as a New York City parent.

We moved into the basement apartment of my mother's house. Mom had moved out to Los Angeles in the fall and was renting out the upstairs (the three floors where I had grown up) to a family that could afford to rent a brownstone in Greenwich Village. The conversation in which I told my mother I was pregnant (after the two miscarriages and after years of her asking when she was getting grandchildren) went like this:

Me: Mom, guess what? I'm pregnant!

Mom (at same time): Hey, guess what? I'm moving to California!

By the time we moved into the basement, her house had been mostly uncared for over the eight months she had been living out West. So when we arrived with the three-week-old Amelia in tow, we had to begin upkeep as well as find our way as parents, plus Greg still needed a job.

I was a new mom, we had no income, we were living in the dark basement apartment of the house I grew up in, my mom was thousands of miles away, and I was desperate for just one good night of sleep. Greg found a job, quit, and found another, better job within the first year we were in New York. I took care of Amelia and the house and eventually got some sleep. By the summer of Amelia's first year, we loved living in the city, had tons of friends—both old and new—and my mom had moved back from her brief fling in Los Angeles.

The next summer, Greg and I decided to move to Brooklyn. Actually, Greg decided to move to Brooklyn even though I wanted to stay in lower Manhattan. I looked at a few terrible, tiny apartments that we couldn't afford before I reluctantly agreed to look in Brooklyn. I spent one day house hunting, and by late that afternoon, I had seen the house I wanted. It was a horrid little house. The smell of cigarettes and cat piss was enough to force me back out the door. Once my eyes adjusted to the dim, grimy lighting inside, I realized that there were almost no redeeming qualities to the place and that everything would have to be torn out. But something about it hit me. And I wanted it. I had a vision as I walked through the dark, faux wood–paneled rooms and into the cramped, filthy kitchen. And the vision was remarkably close to what I ended up with six months and fifty thousand dollars' worth of construction later. Again, this was all about faith; I had to believe that the deal would go through, the contractor would do the job on time and on budget, the roof wouldn't leak, the termites wouldn't eat any more of my basement, and the house would turn out beautifully. And I had to have faith that I would like living in this new part of New York, the outer borough of Brooklyn, and the way-outer neighborhood (more than five subway stops into Brooklyn) of Park Slope.

It wasn't as if I walked around thinking about faith. It is just that I did so many things during the first years of being a parent that seemed to require some kind of inner knowledge, some kind of vague idea that everything would be fine. In looking back, it must have been faith.

We moved into our house in January. I got pregnant again immediately and had the baby the following October. I hated being pregnant again and I was tired and cranky for most of the time during the nine months. Amelia was not interested in napping by the time I was five months into the pregnancy, so I had to bribe her with TV shows, candy, junk food, and anything else I could think of just to get her to let me nap, even if it was only for twenty-five minutes (roughly the time of one PBS cartoon).

It was an odd feeling to come home from the hospital that second time. I was in a home with stability; there were no boxes to pack, Greg had been at the same job for two years, and I had come to love my neighborhood. Still, when I walked in the door holding the tiny new addition to our family I felt fragile and unsure of how to fit two kids into my life. I sat on the couch gripping baby Victor with tears in my eyes. The second time around is worse because you know what you are in for: the sleepless nights, the anxiety over every squawk, the teething, and the constant diapers. And on top of that, the fear over how to serve the needs of the three-year-old who is making her way toward you as you sit and realize that you cannot breathe. I was trying to nurse the baby, and Amelia had to show me her Barbie, and she needed a cup of juice, and asked when were we going to the toy store because she wanted the big sister present she had been promised. I looked up at Greg and burst into tears.

"This is a colossal joke!" I sobbed. "It cannot be done. It is simply not going to work to have two kids. How will it ever work?"

Somehow, over the next few months, it began to work. I learned to nurse and pour juice at the same time. I learned that if babies cry for a few minutes without being bothered, they fall asleep. I learned that a double-wide stroller can fit through most doors, allowing for shopping even with two kids in tow. I spent many days in the winter months sitting in a friend's apartment, leafing through magazines and talking with the other second-time moms about our expanded families, our husbands, and what else we could do with our lives. I wanted to return to my studio and paint again, and by the spring I was interviewing part-time babysitters. Gloria came to work for us that summer. I began to do some work in my studio and I also started preparing to teach at the Metropolitan Museum of Art.

I had wanted to teach art again, something I had done in New Hampshire, but I had not found the right teaching situation since becoming a mother and moving to New York. I did not want a full-time job, I did not want to commute to a college far away, and I just wanted to teach a few days a week with enough time left to paint a little and a lot of time left to be a mom. After not finding anything close to what I wanted, it suddenly came together: my new boss at the museum hired me for three half-days a week, so I would make enough money to pay for the babysitter and let me paint two afternoons a week.

Over the summer, I started putting my lectures together. I was going to be out in the field, teaching in the schools, so I had to figure out which works of art to use and how to use them. I pored over sheets and sheets of slides, wandered the galleries at the museum, and took notes on what I thought would work in the lectures. I thought it would be best to stay away from overtly religious themes, but after a few weeks of looking at the vast collections of the museum, I realized how much art there was that had been made in the name of one god or another. I wasn't sure how it would work for me to have religious art in my lectures, especially in the public schools (what with separation of church and state), and yet it was going to be impossible to avoid it. Most of the art from the ancient times to the nineteenth century was made for religious purposes. Unless all my lectures consisted of images from the impressionists and the modern artists, I would have to include works of religious significance. All the Egyptian, Greek, Roman, and ancient Near Eastern art was made for funerary or devotional ceremony. The medieval and Renaissance works were all about Christianity with so many images of Jesus, Mary, and the many saints. Then there was all the Asian art, with the many Eastern religions represented, and African art, which was almost always made for spiritual purposes.

I ended up including many religious works of art in the lectures I put together. I had to. But I also made sure that most of the major world religions were represented, and I felt I had a good perspective focusing on them as art rather than as religious icons. I would acknowledge that they had great significance to many people, even if those people and their religions no longer existed. I would try to represent the art in its religious and historical context without allowing the context to take over the discussion. Mostly I wanted to get the students to really look at the art for what it is. I would lead them through the way it was made, the reason it was made, and the story behind the work. I would get the students to see the clues that were in the art itself. The closer they looked, the more they would get from the work. After they really related to the work and unlocked the meaning, maybe I could get them to have a better understanding of the many different peoples and religious viewpoints in the world.

I was terrified to teach my first class. I was at Holy Name, a parochial school in Brooklyn, and I started the lecture with an image of a Hindu god on the screen. Weren't all religious people like my in-laws, just waiting to tell me that it is wrong to look at "false idols" or acknowledge other beliefs? Remarkably, the students had studied India and had learned about the god Shiva. I was not going to be thrown out on the street with my heathen slide projector tossed out after me.

In my lectures I showed Shiva, Ganesha, Buddha, many of the Buddhist bodhisattvas (my favorite being Fudo Myo-o, protector of the temple, who is shown as a green-skinned, orange-haired giant with a terrific grimace), as well as the ancient gods of Egypt, Greece, and Assyria, and paintings from the Renaissance featuring Jesus Christ, Mary, even the devil. I had entire lectures that ended up being discussions of how different cultures depicted the gods or religious beliefs in their culture. The more I talked about these religious ideas and the art that came out of them, the more comfortable I became teaching in Catholic schools, yeshivas, and public schools all around New York, filled with devout Jews, Muslims, Hindus, or Jehovah's Witnesses.

I started to see how all the world's religions were connected. One day, while talking with my co-worker Will, we went through some of the many coincidences we had found across the many religions we had encountered in our lectures. We were amazed at them all. What was the real difference, we wondered, between Osiris, the god of the underworld in the ancient Egyptian religion, and the Christian notion of "God in heaven"? Both pass judgment on those who die, Osiris using the scale of justice to measure the goodness in the heart of the deceased to determine if they can enter the afterlife, while God supposedly uses his all-knowing, all-seeing powers to judge and allow entrance into the "Kingdom of Heaven."

"Aren't they all just the same thing?" I asked Will.

"Don't people see that the ideas are so similar? Why is there all this fighting over who is more right?" Will had been raised in the South, so he knew all about right-leaning Christians. "People cling to differences," he said. "They almost seem to find comfort in them."

When I traveled around the city to teach, I was usually alone in a taxi with nobody to talk to about my ideas. So instead I did a lot of thinking, much of it trying to figure out the relationship I had with my in-laws. By this time, they had moved to San Francisco so Jed could work as the music director at a new church there. Before they had moved, we had seen them every so often, and I had come pretty close to forgetting about the slights and insults of the past. I still felt uncomfortable around them some of the time, but usually a vodka on the rocks before they came over would help me deal with the anxiety.

Before they moved, they invited us to go to their church. They wanted us to meet their pastor, a charismatic evangelical preacher who had urged them to "bring the skeptics to the house of God." He was just so important to them, they said, and they really wanted to share his understanding of Christianity with Greg and me. I did not go, though Greg did, and he reported it all back to me. He said the service was just what I thought it would be, and worse, since there were testimonials by "former gays" who, through the love of Christ, had healed themselves of their "horrid, disgusting" lifestyle.

I was glad I had not gone, but the more I heard about the service, the more resentful I was that they had invited me at all. I had no interest in hearing of conversions, nor the offer of eternal life through knowing Jesus, and would not be put in a position where I could be told I was wrong again. I was finding my own kind of faith; my house didn't fall down, and my kids breathed through every night, grew out of clothes, and learned to walk and talk. I had friends, neighbors, and a great community. I looked around at the world and felt that it all made sense without a great ruler in the sky. I was doing just fine on my own and I started to feel a little bit of confidence, in my beliefs and in myself.

chapter 22

bad jew

When I grew up in Chicago, there were no days off from school for the Jewish holidays, however, my mother always took us out of school for the Jewish New Year so we could go apple picking. In New York City, the schools close for both the New Year and Yom Kippur, the Day of Atonement. These holidays always disrupted the flow of getting the kids back to school, and so instead of taking a drive in the country, we usually spent the autumnal high holy days scrambling for a babysitter or, if that failed, calling around for play dates.

The year Amelia was in prekindergarten and Victor was a baby, Rosh Hashanah fell on a day when I had no babysitter. It was a day for me to spend together with the kids, another fun-filled day at the park (the summer, which had not yet officially ended, had been a long string of fun-filled days at the park). We planned to meet up with a bunch of other at-large moms and kids on the far side of our neighborhood. So I packed snacks, fastened the kids into the double stroller, and off we went.

It was a glorious fall day, not too hot but plenty of sun. I was dressed casually, in my park outfit of chinos and a T-shirt.

We set out down 8th Avenue, and I immediately noticed all the well-dressed families out and about. Ah, yes, I realized, well dressed for temple. They were all going to the New Year service. I felt a bit like a fish swimming against the current, since I was walking away from the local synagogue as they were all heading toward it.

I smiled to myself and was glad that I did not have to wear stockings and a fancy dress and sit in a dark temple on such a nice day. But there was a twinge of guilt. Not that I had ever been to services before, not that my mother was asking me if I was going, and if not, why not. My mother had decided to host the Passover seder every year, and she started having a Chanukah party. We were all expected to attend these two celebrations (she still celebrated Christmas, as well, and would celebrate any holiday if it gave her an excuse to throw a party and give her grandchildren more presents). Even though my mother never wanted my sister to go to work on Jewish holidays (you are *Jewish*, she would say, and Gina would roll her eyes), she never expected us to be observant in any way other than attending her parties or maybe eating the right kind of cookie on a certain day.

I had a tradition of always forgetting it was Rosh Hashanah and always cooking pork chops that night. It seemed to happen year after year: I'd be busy cooking away and it would hit me that it was the one night of the year (aside for Yom Kippur) when, as a Jew, I really should be avoiding the pig. It was never clear to me why I felt this way (no one in my family was the least bit kosher) and I always ate the pork chops anyway. But there was always that twinge of guilt, a shadow of a feeling that I should be something I was not.

I thought of the pork chops as the kids and I made our way through the crowds of our well-dressed neighbors. "I should be wearing a T-shirt with "Bad Jew" stamped across it," I thought. My friends all laughed at me when I arrived at the playground and announced my T-shirt idea.

I sat down on the bench and unhooked the children from the stroller. Within minutes, Amelia was running back to me, blood pouring down the back of her dress. She had hit her head on the monkey bars, she was screaming, and I was trying to both calm her down and get a towel on the back of her head to stem the bleeding. Great, I thought, I will be spending my nice, sunny fall day in a place far worse than temple—the emergency room.

I didn't end up in the hospital. But I had a half hour of panic as I tried to figure out what to do. I called the pediatrician, but since it was a Jewish holiday, Dr. Seth was out of the office and so was his usual replacement doctor, Dr. Schwartz. So I was on the phone to Dr. Ling, whom I had never even heard of before, and he was trying to tell me what to do. I could barely hear him over the wails of my bleeding daughter, and when I tried to get a better look at the cut, to see if the edges were pulling away (in which case, according to Dr. Ling, she needed stitches), she screamed and flinched.

Suddenly my "Bad Jew" joke didn't seem so funny. Was that old feeling from first grade slipping back into my brain? Was God punishing me—and this time my daughter—for my nontemple-attending, pork chop–eating ways?

A friend who had been a nurse before she became a mother showed up and advised me to keep the cut clean and dry and to not bother with stitches. Amelia was greatly relieved to find out that she would be spared a trip to the emergency room, and I was happy to pass on having to hold down a screaming four-year-old as doctors stitched her head. We spent a quiet afternoon back at home, and I never did have that T-shirt made.

But I couldn't help wondering why I always went back to the idea that I was being punished by God. The longer I was married to my firmly atheist husband, the more I began to sway that way. I didn't believe in God. And if I didn't believe in him, then how could I be punished by him? It was just the child side of my brain talking when I had those thoughts.

This sway toward nonbelief made it hard for me to find meaning in the more religious of the big American holidays. Once I was a mom, once I was in charge of the house, once I had to decide what was to become a family tradition, I really had to look hard at what I felt was at the core of these holidays. Many of them had God at the core, and I had to find ways around that. Could I find meaning in these God holidays without God in my life?

Easter was easy; we ate some chocolate eggs, end of story. We did nothing for Good Friday, the Feast of the Assumption, Ash Wednesday, Sukkoth, or many other holidays that had New York City parking rules suspended for them but no deep connection to American culture. My mother had taken on Chanukah with a party and potato pancakes. Christmas was the real challenge, and I had long despised the holiday for its pressures, expectations, obligations, and for the disappointment it always delivered.

I had started to dislike Christmas after my parents got divorced. Without all the trappings of the holiday to distract me, I began to remember all the fights and bad times that had ever occurred around December: the year my father threw the gift my mother gave him out the back window of our house, the tears because my mother had not gotten the nice piece of jewelry she thought she was getting, the time that we all spent the midnight hour of the night before Christmas screaming at one another. There had been plenty of good times too, in Chicago and then in New York, with friends and family, presents, and fun. But for the ten years between the disintegration of my parents' marriage and me having my own family, I mostly ignored Christmas. I even had a few years of devout paganism when I would only celebrate the solstice. I saw the celebration of days getting longer again as the real reason for the season. But the kids made Christmas inevitable (I did consider keeping to my solstice celebrations, but one friend told me that my kids would be tagged as weird if we didn't do one of the two major holidays of the season). As I began to celebrate Christmas with my own family, I began to like it again. I liked going to visit Santa, decorating the house, buying gifts, and having parties.

The first step toward Christmas comfort was to wrestle Christmas away from my mother's control. Although Mom was "Jewish," she had always celebrated Christmas and loved the holiday. She also felt that she owned the holiday, since, for the first few years of Amelia's life, we would spend the holiday at her country house with her fully in charge of presents, meals, and the guest list. Those celebrations always ended with me being in a confused state. I was uncomfortable with the numerous presents, the huge overflow of food on the table, and the seemingly endless supply of distant family members and acquaintances who were

invited to join us. It seemed like too much, first Chanukah
and then Christmas. Why couldn't we just pick one?
Chanukah would have made me feel like a better Jew, but I
did not feel that it meant as much to me as Christmas did
because it was not in our family vocabulary of holidays from
way back. So the problem was that I couldn't fit into the
Jewish holiday, but I couldn't quite feel comfortable with
the Christian one either.

Once I had my own house, I wanted to be there for
December 25. I wanted to plan the meals and be in control
of the gifts and the guest lists. The first year I "had"
Christmas, I decided I wanted it to be about family, togetherness, and sharing. So I invited my *whole* family. My
divorced parents and my sister were there. Everyone was
told to "just get along," and they did. My three-year-old and
my infant son were the center of the day, and in the end it
was a bright spot on the winter's dull horizon.

One year, when Amelia was five, we went to see the
Radio City Christmas Spectacular. Victor was still too young
to sit in a seat in the dark, even for dancing reindeer and bell-
shaking Santas, but Amelia loved it. We laughed through all
the overblown silliness of the sets, the costumes, the perfectly orchestrated Rockettes, and the lighthearted cheer that
it cast on the Christmas season. Then, after the stage had been
cleared of all things secular and giddy, the lights came back
on slowly. There, in the middle of the stage, was a hill. On
the hill were goats and cows, maybe an ox, a few camels, and
in the middle was the holy family. It was the Nativity Scene,
live on stage. I had not expected the show to turn so religious.
I had somehow missed it in the program listing. "Well," I
thought, "after all, Jesus is the reason for the season."

On the taxi ride home, I questioned Amelia. "What did you think of the last part, the part with the baby and all the animals?"

"Oh," she said, "that was the baby Jesus. He was born in the manger and is the son of God."

I was blown away. How did she know that? She was only in kindergarten, and I had not yet had any discussions with her on the subject. I calmly asked where she had learned all this information.

"From the song 'Away in the Manger.' Miss Barker taught it to us in school. She said that Jesus was born on Christmas Day and that is why we all get presents. You know I still want Velvet Barbie for Christmas, right?"

"Right, and we'll go see Santa next week to tell him." I was relieved to shift the focus to Santa and away from Christ the Lord.

It seemed odd to secularize the most reverent of the Christian high holy days, but that was what I did. That was what my family had always done. We never set foot in a church, we were happy to have Christmas be about presents, with Santa and Bing Crosby. My mother served ham on Christmas Eve every year in full shirking of her Jewish heritage. As I sat in the Radio City Music Hall watching the baby Jesus come to life before my eyes, I panicked: "What do all the Jews do during this part?" And it took me a few moments of a racing heart and sweaty palms before I remembered that any Jew who would be offended by the Living Nativity Scene would not be going to a Christmas Spectacular in the first place.

After many years, I decided to embrace the true meaning of Christmas by acknowledging the birth of Jesus. I bought a tiny crèche scene, with the baby Jesus and the animals, at the Christmas Market in Piazza Navona the year we spent the holiday in Italy. In a Catholic country, there is no denying the root of the season, with crèche scenes everywhere, and I had become fond of the holy family. We now live in a house with a menorah on one end of the piano and a crèche scene at the other in a perfect balance of the heritages we come from.

In the spring, of course, there is the same confusion. Every year brings the most holy of holy days in the Christian calendar right next to the holiday that even the least religious Jew will celebrate. We rarely celebrated Passover when I was a child, but we did celebrate Easter, at least until the year the holiday ended bitterly when I was about ten, and my sister spent Easter weekend at her friend Amy's house. Gina and Amy had been in kindergarten together and had stayed friends even though the Larsen family had moved out of Chicago to a big farm in southern Illinois. I was rather shocked when, on Easter Eve, I wandered into the kitchen, expecting to find Mom boiling eggs and making the vinegar and food coloring dye, and instead found the room dark. My parents were relaxing in the living room: Mom was reading and drinking a glass of wine, and Dad was listening to his jazz records.

"Hey!" I said. "What about the Easter eggs and the baskets and the Easter Bunny and all that?"

My parents looked at me and smiled. "You are too old for all that stuff now," they said. "You know there is no Easter Bunny, so let's just forget the whole thing."

I cried until they agreed to let me blow an egg out of its shell (as I had seen on *Zoom*) and then paint it. I didn't get a basket of candy the next day, and when Gina came home with enough candy to fill a pillowcase, I went back to crying until Mom and Dad made her share her bounty with me.

I've never really celebrated Easter since (just pass me a marshmallow egg and I'm happy), but the Jewish celebration of spring and rebirth seemed to be a holiday worth celebrating. I just had not figured out how to get it right. I always remembered how much I had enjoyed the long-ago seder with the Manns in Boston with the mix I longed for: family gathering, tradition, and connection. In the years that followed, I had gone to the occasional seder but never liked any as much as the Mann family affair.

After one particularly long and boring seder at the Weiss house (they were also old family friends, but aside from being long and dull, their seder was also very religious), we decided that Mom would host next year's seder. She cooked all the proper foods and set a nice table, but she didn't get the word part right. She had bookmarks and notes all over her Haggadah, but none of it made much sense. It was a family gathering, but there was no connection.

The next year, Mom tried again, but she and I had a big fight on seder night. It started out as a simple misunderstanding about scheduling a sleepover for the kids and ended up as a blowup over many other things, including her hap hazard seders. I was determined to do my own seder the next year.

Mom came to my house but was not happy about relinquishing another holiday to my domain. I wanted to show her how to do it right, so I cooked a great meal and even wrote my own Haggadah. It included only the best parts of the seder, like the history, the explanations of traditions, and any part that involved an activity like dipping, dripping, or asking. I worked on my Haggadah for weeks, cutting and pasting parts from different versions of the book I found, and in the end I had exactly what I wanted. I took great pains to have God's name mentioned only five times and then only in the story of Moses, where it could not be left out. I had also condensed the entire ritual down to six pages, so it was very kid-friendly.

The seder finally made sense to me and helped me convey the most important parts of the holiday to my children, the parts about freedom and togetherness. I served the matzoh ball soup with "floaters" (matzo balls that are light and buoyant, the most difficult kind to make) and I thought about my "Bad Jew" T-shirt. I didn't feel like a bad Jew anymore. I felt good about the way I was celebrating holidays with my family and I felt happy that I could embrace the different heritages that made us what we were.

chapter 23

take it back

I wanted family to be an important part of my life, but I found myself struggling with it on all fronts. My mother and I had a bad summer, and at the end of it, I joked that I had spent the summer getting a divorce from my mom. I wanted closeness and togetherness, but I was getting invasion and intrusion.

My husband's family was also causing problems. His sister had a baby that fall (a boy named Jacob), and she and Jed pretty much fell apart during their first year as parents. The first months were especially difficult for them, and they liked to share the misery with those around them. We were not exactly around them since they were still living in San Francisco, but we were going to see them during their Christmas visit back East. We were excited for them to have a baby, since we hoped it would give us something new to connect over. I thought I could be the helpful sister-in-law, the one they would call on for her level head and good, commonsense advice.

They were staying with Jed's family in New Jersey, so we arranged to meet them in Manhattan on the Sunday after Christmas. They were planning to spend a day in the city

and go to their old church, which was around the corner
from my mother's apartment (she had moved into the downstairs of our old house in Greenwich Village). Mom was out
of town for the week, so we decided to meet the new family
there. I figured we'd see the new baby, have lunch, send
them off to church, and then take a nice walk around the old
neighborhood.

Instead we spent most of the day waiting. New parents
never accurately judge how long everything takes, and Jed
and Megan were always running behind schedule before
they had a baby, so we should not have been surprised when
they walked in the door three hours late. They walked in
looking stressed and miserable, and the visit was strained
and tense. Something was obviously wrong; Megan kept
crying but would not tell us why. I tried to talk to her while
she nursed the baby in my mom's bedroom. I wanted to help,
but she would barely look at me, much less talk to me.

Jed admitted that they were not having a very good trip;
they were worried about the baby and his weight gain, they
were not sleeping at all, and his family was trying to be
helpful but was giving a lot of unwanted advice. I was about
to suggest that they give the baby some formula, or that they
try some tricks I knew about calming babies, but I clamped
my mouth shut and smiled sympathetically instead. I was
not keen on giving unwanted advice.

They left after Megan had fed the baby (which took
hours); she was still upset and crying, and then we didn't
hear from them again for months. I felt terrible for them, as
I always felt bad when new parents are unhappy. I had been
a fairly upbeat new mom, even with a move two weeks into
it and an unemployed husband. I sent Megan a book as a

feel-better gift. It was *Operating Instructions* by Anne Lamott. I had found it to be a great new-mom read, since it covered the ups and downs of the first year of motherhood in a way I had found both funny and accurate. I thought it would be a perfect book for Megan to read. Since Anne Lamott talked a lot about her Christian faith and how it helped get her through, I thought it would be a good match for that part of Megan's life, too.

I never heard about the book or the note I attached. I knew that Jed and Megan were parenting book junkies, but they never called to say they had gotten the book, much less that they had enjoyed the read. I was upset. My plans for connecting with my sister-in-law as moms-in-arms, muddling through it together, were dashed. I would have to be content with the quick phone calls and the uncomfortable silences I got if I offered anything that was even close to advice. Anecdotes, sharing an experience, or mentioning a friend's solution to a common problem were unwelcome from me.

I was disappointed, but I couldn't dwell on it. I had other things to worry about: we had purchased a new house in Brooklyn, the old house was still on the market, Amelia's public school was undergoing a change of administration, and I was still learning the ropes in my second year of teaching.

By the following Christmas, we had moved into the new house. It was right around the corner from the old house, but it was bigger, nicer, and did not have termites. We were happy once we were moved in, but the move itself ended up being a small nightmare. We had sold our house two weeks before the new one was ready in September, so we put our stuff in storage and moved in with my dad. I commuted to Brooklyn with the kids for school and killed time while trying not to be completely stressed. Our lawyer was supposed to call with the closing date on the new house, and day after day slipped by with me sitting in a coffee shop, staring at the tiny blue cell phone, willing it to ring.

Christmas that year was busy. My cousins from Spain were in town, staying with my mother, and so I had a big dose of family on my side. Greg's mother had spent a week with us in early December, and I had spent most of the week with her, so I had gotten a big dose of family on his side, too. By the time the New Year rolled around, I was ready for the family visits to end and I wanted time to really settle into the new house. But we still had to schedule a visit with Jed, Megan, and Jacob, who was now a one-year-old. They were back East for the yearly Christmas visit, and although they were planning a trip into New York City, they were reluctant to come "all the way" to Brooklyn to see us. I was unwilling to meet them anywhere else after last year's three-hour wait. I could picture sitting at a diner with a two-year-old and a five-year-old waiting for my in-laws until my kids had ripped the place apart and we were thrown out on the cold winter street.

Since we had no plans with the in-laws, Greg and I spent the eve of "Y2K" at home, eating fancy foods in front of the TV, watching as the New Year dawned across the world, to no ill effect. We had heard about the horrible things that might go wrong with the changeover from 1999 to 2000. When we went to sleep, minutes after the ball dropped in Times Square, our electricity was still on, our phones still worked, and clean water still ran out of our taps.

We tried to arrange a Brooklyn dinner with Greg's sister in the first days of 2000, but it all fell apart. They wanted to come in the middle of the day, and I was inviting them for the early evening. It would have been easier to accommodate their needs, but I was fed up with the needs my various family members and I needed a normal, uninterrupted day. So I said no. I said that they could not come in the middle of the day but that they were welcome to come at five o'clock. I told them that it would be lovely to see them, to show them the new house, to have the kids play together, to enjoy a glass of wine and eat together as a family. They said if they couldn't come at one in the afternoon (so that Jacob could take a nap at my house), they couldn't come at all. The conversation turned nasty; they were not getting their way and they were upset. But I held firm to my refusal to blow my day.

By saying no to them, I made them angry. By making them angry, I opened the relationship to scrutiny. I started thinking about why I was unwilling to compromise my day (it was only one day, after all, and I could have made up the time in my studio or studying for my lectures). I thought about how slighted I had felt over the years, but especially in the last year. I had to acknowledge the lack of connection, even as parents.

They returned to the West Coast without seeing us, and a week later we received a letter. When I saw they had written us, I was actually excited. Although I knew it could say they were disappointed and hurt that I had not been more flexible and sensitive to the needs of their family, I was still hopeful. Maybe it would be a thank-you note for the Anne Lamott book or an apology for making us wait three hours last year. Maybe they were reaching out, making a connection, which is all I really wanted. Instead, they explained that once they arrived home, they reached the conclusion that the relationship they had with us was shallow, based on the fact that they could not "be Christian" when they were around us. They ended the letter with a long explanation of why Christ is the only truth. So instead of a connection, I got a religious treatise that outlined the reasons, in black and white, why I was wrong.

After fuming for a few days about what to do and what to say, Greg phoned Jed and Megan to tell them how we felt. I hovered in the background as Greg tried to explain that we were angry and upset by their letter. They were surprised at our furious reaction. They thought they were bringing healing and closeness by writing so honestly to us. Greg passed the phone to me and they asked what they could do to prove that they cared about the relationship. They wanted to know how they could make a gesture toward healing.

I asked if they recalled the conversation that we had the day before Arlene's wedding all those years ago. I asked if they recalled telling me I was wrong. They reluctantly admitted that they may have said such a thing, but they were sure they had said it in a loving way.

"Well, the damage you did to our relationship back then has finally come back to haunt us," I said. "I tried to bury it and I tried to forget it, but this letter and this insistence that we put religion—your religion—at the core of our familial friendship is a problem. I want to connect with you over other things in life. You want to be able to 'be Christian.' I don't care what you are, be whatever makes you happy. But if you want to know what you can do to prove to me that you value my friendship, I'll tell you. Take back what you said about me being wrong.

"Accept me for who I am and tell me that you won't try to change me, convert me, or convince me anymore," I demanded. "Tell me that I am as right in my beliefs as you are in yours. Say that I have every right to believe as I please."

They could not possibly do that, they explained, because taking back the statement "You are wrong!" would mean that I was not wrong, when, in fact, I *was* wrong. Saying otherwise would have gone against the firm foundations of their beliefs. And how, oh, how, could I even think of asking them to forsake their beliefs? Didn't I have *any* respect for them and for their church? How could they forsake the very cornerstone of what they believed in?

So there we were, me with my open mind and them with their absolutism. There were discussions for months following the letter, but they always seemed to end in the same stalemate. Each hour-long try at getting them to agree to disagree ended the same way: they were right, they had God on their side, the Bible is the true word of God, and they were sure that they were set for eternity while I was clearly not. So I always ended up wrong.

They did respect me, they claimed. They weren't saying that they were better than I was, and they admitted that I was good at a lot of things, like cooking and art. They liked me— they *loved* me—even with all my faults. And don't worry, they told me, all humans have faults, all humans are imperfect and broken. That is why God gave us his only son, to ensure that in spite of our failures we can still be saved. But they wouldn't say that I was right, or even that I had a right to believe in my own way. I was always, eternally, wrong.

It did not even vaguely occur to them that they were

caught in a big double standard. All they knew was that they were "right" and therefore should be able to say so. And they could say it joyfully, with holy hosts singing around their heads, no less. And as for me, well, as always, the sooner I realized the errors of my ways the sooner I could get on the track toward walking with Jesus. I should have hung up right then and never looked back. But it was not so easy. The pull of family was strong. The need to make it all okay again was strong, since I had been the one to say no and start the fight, after all. The need to stay in the conflict and try, again and again, to be heard was strong. I could not hang up on them; I had to continue to argue.

I was thoroughly caught in the web. I had a deep need to be heard and understood. This was a tall order for people like Jed and Megan. It was a tall order for people like my parents, as well. They never really liked to hear me out. They often dismissed me (or my ideas) as ridiculous, strident, or misguided. It occurred to me that what I was really doing was playing out dramas from my past experiences in the fight I was having with my in-laws. When they told me I was wrong, refused to hear what I had to say, and continued to espouse an irrational worldview, it somehow connected with me deeply. Another person would have been able to laugh it all off. Another person could have dismissed them as quickly and easily as they had dismissed me. But I had to take it on. I needed the connection—any connection—and this fight was all I had.

It was exhausting to fight with them, especially since there was a three-hour time difference and we ended up staying up late to talk on the phone. We were getting nowhere. It kept going around and around, and never once did we discuss how it all started. Never once did we talk about how I said no to them, nor did we touch on the disappointment or anger that it caused. Instead it was about me and Greg trying to get them to accept the fact that we were nonbelievers, or them trying to get us to become believers.

By the spring, after Greg's mother and grandmother had become embroiled in the fight, Greg and I snapped out of it, saw the fight as damaging the family, and called Megan and Jed to end the fight. We apologized, even though we were not sure exactly what we had done that called for an apology other than saying no back in January. But what the hell, saying "I'm sorry for any hurt I have caused" wasn't so hard. They said they forgave us and hoped for a real relationship.

I had to laugh as I hung up on the final night of what came to be known as "The Fight." I wondered what they could mean by "real relationship." I thought that real relationships came out of trust, fondness, and caring. I had been told I was wrong and had then been told I was wrong for asking to be told I wasn't wrong. I was not feeling trust or fondness for them, although I was sure that we would have a relationship: a strained, uncomfortable, and obligatory one.

chapter 24

god bless america

I was sorry that I had stirred the pot with Greg's family, that I had caused so much trouble, that I had asked for tolerance where it could not be given. I had apologized and had been forgiven, but I was not over my feelings of anger and frustration. The fire was out, but the embers were smoldering. It was not easy to see my in-laws. The visits following the fight were awkward.

I thought that seeing them in neutral territory would be best, so we met up with them in Upstate New York, where Megan worked during the summer. The visit was without incident, but it seemed shallow and tentative. Next, I went to their house in San Francisco. I thought that meeting on their turf would improve the situation, but it did not. It was Easter, and the deeply religious significance of the holiday made me more than a little uncomfortable. Everyone seemed withdrawn and cautious, so there was lots of idle chitchat, but nothing I would call a relationship-building conversation. I invited them to my house, but they could never make it. Whenever they were in New York, they were too busy to come to Brooklyn to see us.

Meanwhile, I continued to wage a battle with my side of the family. My mother and I really hit rock bottom the summer following the fight with my in-laws. We had our own fight, which wasn't just big. It was a monster. It lasted for the entire summer, with small cease-fires giving way to big dramatic firefights. I was saying no to her, too. And she was not at all happy about it. My mother is a woman who gets her way; if she can't get it by asking, she'll try bribing, and if she can't win at the bribe game, then she resorts to anger. She felt left out and rejected much of the time because I was saying no to her requests and invitations. She felt edged out of her grandchildren's lives and was depressed and angry that she could not have unlimited access and free reign with them.

At the same time, I was feeling hemmed in. I had to report my decisions and activities to Mom at all times, and she had no problem telling me when she thought what I was doing was the wrong thing. We fought on the phone and we fought in person. We fought when we were out on Long Island (while visiting my sister who had bought a house in the Hamptons) and we fought in Hillsdale (where she had given me her house for a week to use alone with the kids but then, at the last minute, had decided she would join us). I was trying to cut apron strings, which wound around my neck each time I thought I was free. In the end, they wound around my kids, through my marriage, and seemed to weave through too much of my life.

At the end of the summer, after the week I spent at her house when I thought she was not going to be there, we had a terrible fight. We screamed, yelled, and swore. There were accusations, threats, and all manner of hotheaded, irrational statements that extended into the wee hours of the morning. Finally the fight ended with tears, apologies, and promises of reconciliation.

The morning after this blowup, I left the kids with Mom and headed to Boston to meet Greg and attend a friend's wedding. I was exhausted and conflicted about driving away from the scene of the fight and leaving my mother with my two children while there were so many unresolved issues. She would never take her anger at me out on her grandchildren, but I felt scared that too many horrible things had been said, too much anger had been allowed to come out too fast and too furiously. The rush of a year's worth of pent-up frustration was almost enough to flatten me. Somehow, I said good-bye to Mom and the kids and drove across the Mass Turnpike, crying and worrying about the strange dynamic of needing independence while asking for help with the kids for the weekend.

Greg and I had a great time in Boston. It was fun to see our old friends at the wedding, and we also got some much-needed alone time. I drove back across the state of Massachusetts two days later with a hopeful attitude. Maybe things could get better after hitting the lowest point. I was not sure that this philosophy of optimism was working with my in-laws, but I was certain that it would work with Mom. I just had to prove to her that I really was a grown-up. I knew that my mother had a hard time seeing me in my present state of adulthood. To the rest of the world, I was a mother of two, an educator, an artist, a homeowner, and a productive member of society—but to Mom I was still a malleable, moody teenager.

School started and I was looking forward to the autumn.

I had two kids in full-day school thanks to a full-day prekindergarten program for Victor. September 11, 2001, was the first day that I had all to myself. It was supposed to be Victor's first day of eight-thirty to three o'clock school, and I was looking forward to the time with plans of cleaning the house and getting organized for the school year ahead. By nine o'clock, the day was ruined, the world was forever changed, and I was sitting in my living room watching the news and crying.

Luckily, no one in our family or in our immediate circle of friends was harmed. But our city was in a state of unsettled fear and sadness. It became hard to get up in the morning because we knew we would face more bad news, more dead, more missing who would never be found, more destruction, and constant disruption of our lives. The only response we could come up with was to be calm with measured, carefully set routines. We sent the kids off to school every day. We went to work. We tried to stay positive and find our way through what had occurred so suddenly, through this event that had changed us forever.

It was very difficult to make or receive phone calls in the hours that followed the collapse of the Twin Towers. But by the end of the day, we had checked in with all our family members and with many of our friends. I was home all day, except for those few minutes I was at school to get the children after the ash from the collapsed buildings stopped raining down on our neighborhood. Greg, who had seen the second plane hit the building from the elevated track of the F train, was stuck in Manhattan and had to walk home. While I waited for him, I sat at the dining room table and watched burned bits of paper float down through the smoke that blew overhead and spoke to anyone who managed to get through on the phone.

I had spoken to my family many times throughout the day and was on the phone with my mother when the first tower came crashing down. I was almost hysterical when my best friend, Deborah, finally got through to me. But by the time Greg's mom reached me, I was calm, eerily calm. Arlene was so relieved that we were all okay that she cried. After that first hour, I didn't cry for a long time. I couldn't start, since I might not be able to stop.

The months following that day were very odd. I had a drink (or two or three) most nights; it was the best way to take the anxiety back a few notches without a prescription. I cleaned the house and cleared out closets and organized things as often as possible so I could feel more in control of my surroundings. I threw the junk mail away before I got it into the house (anthrax) and I avoided Midtown and Times Square (dirty bombs). I thought of moving to a small, safe town like Great Barrington, Massachusetts.

After that day, I knew one thing for sure: the feeling all around was intensely patriotic. On September 11, no one on my block had an American flag in front of their house; on September 12, five neighbors were flying Old Glory. I did not own an American flag, so I made one with my kids. I have always loved my country's flag, right down to its humble beginnings with Betsy Ross stitching by candlelight. We painted the stripes and used a cookie cutter to trace the stars. It was cute, and I hung it in the front window for a few days. But I started to get the feeling that the flag had other meanings beyond showing allegiance to the good ole U. S. of A. I started to see flags that had writing on them. "God

Bless America," the flags proclaimed. It was as if patriotism had developed fresh ties to religion overnight. I didn't want my flag to mean that I believed in God.

I knew that the link between God and America had always been strong, but now the relationship seemed to have new energy. There were religious people in our country who felt they had the corner on the grief market, who spoke of the tragedy as if they were the only ones who could understand it or explain it, and who used the situation to further their own religious agenda. Some, like Jerry Falwell, claimed that God was punishing New York for all the sinners and anti-Christians who live here. Others said that God had a plan, although Mayor Giuliani admitted that he had no idea what that plan could be. I felt very American, but seeing the members of the Senate sing "God Bless America" on the steps of the Capitol did not make my heart throb with warm feelings for my country. I deeply resented this blurring of the separation of church and state. It made me feel like an outsider for not thinking that God might bless our country in some special way, even as the smoke from the collapsed towers still drifted over my house and the numbers of dead still were not tallied. How could I be a good American and a nothing, a nonbeliever, at the same time?

Thomas Jefferson must have thought it was possible, and yet his ideals seemed to have vanished during the televised prayers by our leading politicians. I was sick of George Bush and his smug certainty that we were God's chosen people and that prayer and God's grace would get us through this terrible time. His speeches during September and October had the zeal of a religious fanatic. I knew that he thought he could talk to God and that it was the same God who directed him to invade Afghanistan and later, Iraq. I knew that he would never respect me as a nonbeliever. He was like my in-laws: righteous, intolerant, and arrogant.

During that fall, I sat through the television news with gritted teeth, ever more frustrated that the only words of comfort anyone could find had to do with God. At baseball games I stood during the seventh-inning stretch when they played the now-required "God Bless America," but only because I would have gotten punched if I hadn't. I refused to sing along and I only took off my hat if someone yelled at me. It isn't the national anthem, I wanted to shout back, so I don't have to take off my hat. But by the seventh inning, those baseball fans have had a lot of beer, and it is better not to be confrontational. So off came the hat, with teeth clenched and anger rising in my throat.

Anger was an ordinary part of my day. Until I realized that although everything had changed, I still had every right to be myself and to believe in whatever I chose. I started thinking about what it was I did believe and about what words did bring comfort to me.

I watched our city fall apart and then slowly come together. And I didn't think any of the "getting through" had anything to do with divine intervention. Never before had I felt so strongly that it was people who occupied the core of my faith. I watched as memorial services and funerals marked the end of life for some and the continuation for others. I watched as communities grew out of the ashes, were rebuilt, and became strong. I was sad and yet hopeful that we would all, somehow, be alright in the end.

Megan called me on 9/11 and then again a few days later to ask if she could send me something from her church. It was a Christian response to the tragedy, and she thought it might help, or at least be an interesting read. I told her to send it along, as long as it wasn't going to say that we had deserved the attack for being an immoral city made up of nonbelievers and deviants. I was interested in different responses to this event, since at that point I was still in shock and still working on what my own response would be.

As I expected, I read and dismissed the *Christian Response to 9/11* sent to me by Megan. But it was an opportunity for me to be clear and tell her that it was of no help at all to me. I suddenly felt at ease admitting to her that I simply did not get anything from Christianity. I said thanks for the effort, but turning to God is not at all what I think will get us through. I told her that the ability to heal, the human ability to get better, was the only thing I could believe in. I told her that the hardest part for me was in those early days and weeks following the attack, as we waited for the healing to begin. After the first few days, I knew that there would be no more hope of finding survivors, but I knew that as life picked up and went on, as families suffering from loss would have to get back into their daily routines, then I would start to feel better. Then my faith would become renewed.

It was one month to the day after 9/11 when Greg and I went to the play-off game between the Yankees and the Oakland Athletics at Yankee Stadium in the Bronx. That afternoon, I decided to walk downtown, below Canal Street, for the first time since the buildings had fallen. The streets had been closed for most of the month, and there was still no traffic as I neared the site. I walked the route I had always walked when I used to head down to the World Trade Center as a teenager. It was a frequent destination whenever out-of-town guests were visiting. We would set out from the brownstone on 12th Street and head downtown, through the heart of Greenwich Village and then through SoHo and TriBeCa, ending with a milkshake at the top of the Twin Towers.

As I walked from SoHo that day, I thought about how this downtown was so different from the downtown of my younger years, and before long, I was standing on the northern perimeter of Ground Zero. I couldn't really see much, since there were big white sheets hoisted across the streets so that the sightlines into the wreckage were blocked. Police, firefighters, and construction workers went in and out of checkpoints. Many people like me, people who had come to see, were standing, craning their necks to try to catch a glimpse.

By that time, I had seen the images on TV thousands of times, as had the rest of the country and the world, but this was different. This was my city. I had a high school friend who had lived on Chambers Street; her house had very little parental supervision, so I spent a lot of time there. Now Chambers Street was part of Ground Zero (a term I quickly came to dislike; I preferred to call it "the site" or "where the Towers were"). I sat on a low wall across from the white sheets and the checkpoints and I felt like crying. I felt as if I didn't belong there. I was a gawker, a rubbernecker, just here to see the damage. I slowly started to walk back uptown to meet Greg and get on the D train to get to the Bronx for the eight o'clock game. I turned a few blocks uptown and looked back at where I had been. From there I could see over the sheets that had blocked my view. From there I could see the utter destruction, the pile of twisted metal, and the excavators working at the top of the pile, pulling away tiny little mouthfuls from the huge mound of wreckage. I turned and continued uptown, looking back now and then until the street turned a bit and I no longer had a clear view.

We got to Yankee Stadium in time for the "Star-Spangled Banner." I had never heard people actually sing along with the national anthem, but tonight, all fifty-six thousand fans seemed to be joining in. After it was done, there was immense silence, the kind that can only exist in a packed arena, a silence that is ready to burst, a tense and swallowed kind of silence. There was a huge American flag on the field, and an eagle flew across the flag to home plate. Someone yelled, "God bless the USA!" and the crowd erupted into cheers.

There was something strange about feeling so much unity in New York City. Maybe at other baseball parks in other parts of the country there is always that feeling, but in New York, we are individuals first, New Yorkers second, and Americans third. Or it used to be that way, before they flew planes into our tallest buildings. The crowd began to cheer, "USA! USA!" until the Yankees took the field and the loud rock-and-roll drowned out the patriotic chants.

The Yankees lost that night, but they went on to win the play-offs before they got beaten by the Diamondbacks in the World Series. I thought that the Arizona team should have let the New York team win, since we needed it more than they did. Watching baseball became my tranquilizer. It made me feel normal, safe, and happy. For those few hours a night, I could forget the pain of loss that blanketed the city. I could forget about the endless memorial services, the fire stations all draped in black bunting, the widows, and the grief. I didn't rerun the Towers falling, over and over, in my mind's eye.

Baseball season ended and the holidays set in, but I barely remember Christmas that year. I remember buying gifts and wrapping things and getting a tree, but it was all done as if I had been sleepwalking. There was joy; there was merriment, but it was forced and uncomfortable. We were not supposed to be having fun yet, since the dust from the Towers had not even settled. Greg left his office some evenings with the smell of burning flesh and metal still hanging in the air. There were still memorial services and "Portraits of Grief," little obituaries of each person who had died, each day in the *New York Times.*

We went to California for the week after Christmas. We drove up and down the state, visiting Greg's family and staying in cheap motels. It was strange to be so far away from New York. It was weird to feel that the whole country owned what had happened in our city. Even as far away as California, there were cars and trucks with American flags on the antennae and "FDNY" painted on the back windshields. There were billboards and T-shirts with patriotic slogans and messages for New York. There were Christmas trees with red, white, and blue lights (as there had been in Rockefeller Center that year, too). And there, on the piano in Greg's mother's living room, was a small sculpture of Santa holding the American flag.

When I think back on the trip out West that year, I recall how unhappy I was. Nothing was going as planned. We were all sick, it rained, and seeing family wasn't turning out to be the reaffirming experience we had hoped for. If family was so important to me, then why wasn't I having a good time? I was seeing the family, I was spending time visiting with them all, and yet I felt distant and isolated from everyone.

They all had their own problems—a new baby, an elderly mother—and we arrived with sullen reports from the city, full of sadness and worry.

We tried to feel good about having made the trip. We did see the old folks, which included Greg's three living grandparents who were all nearing ninety. And we saw the new baby, Jacob's brother, Jeremy. We saw him, but we didn't get to touch him due to our sniffles and hacking coughs. The best thing was that the calendar no longer had 2001 at the top; the year was over and we were all glad to see it go. It was a year of terror, death, and destruction. The rebirth was yet to come. But in our hopeful, human hearts, we sensed that the New Year could bring healing, and through that healing we would be able to start resuming our lives.

chapter 25

mommy, what do
we believe in?

i was driving in Manhattan one day. I signaled to make a
right turn onto Broadway. There were many people all
around the car, including pedestrians, other drivers, and a
bus at the intersection full of riders. There were huge adver-
tisements on the side of the bus, blown-up pictures of
celebrities—people—staring down at me. I had to wait to
make the turn, since the crosswalk was still crowded. I
looked all around me and felt the strong presence of the
people. My car windows were rolled up. I didn't hear, touch,
or smell anyone; it was a different kind of sense at work. The
strong presence was that each person—right there on the
street at that very moment in time—was thinking of something, was remembering, feeling, forming an idea. It was as
if I could feel all those brains at work. I could feel the energy
that made all those people individuals. Each person in the
world has his own story, thoughts, and internal life. It
seemed overwhelming, and I had to remind myself to
breathe. I took in a deep breath, and the crosswalk cleared. I
put my foot to the gas pedal and took the turn down
Broadway. The moment passed, I turned on the radio, and
drove home.

After the Towers fell, people suddenly noticed each other on the street or on the subway. Eyes would meet and feelings would be exchanged in a blink: "I'm all right, how are you?" "Can you believe this has happened?" "It's okay, we're all scared." New York was suddenly filled with people: people trying to hold on and get through, people who were hurting and crying and needing comfort, and people who were able to give, even if they were only giving a moment of themselves.

Maybe it was that kind of collective generosity of spirit that made it hard to believe that Megan and Jed did not call us when they were in New York that winter. Maybe we felt that we had tried hard to connect with family, and we wanted family to reach out to us in return. They came to the East Coast for a family visit, to see Jed's family, but they did not tell us they were coming. They did not call when they were in New York for their usual few days. We were stunned, hurt, and angry by this oversight. When we told them how we felt, they were shocked. They had a list of excuses about why they hadn't called. Excuses made us feel worse.

So we reentered the conflict with them. This time, though, it had nothing to do with religion or philosophy, it had to do with dashed expectations and selfishness. They couldn't see why we were angry (it was just a phone call), we couldn't allow the sham of friendship to go on (if you really wanted to be "friends," you would have at least called). The second phase of the fight escalated, with nasty e-mails, accusations, and furious denials on both sides, until we stopped speaking to them altogether. After years of trying to make the troubled relationship work and keep the family together, I had failed entirely. Now it was worse than it had ever been; we had actually stopped all communication. This bothered me and kept me awake at night. How could I not be speaking to members of my own family? Well, members of my husband's family, but I didn't want to be the kind of person who wasn't speaking to her sister-in-law.

My in-laws were sure of what they believed in. They had millions of other people who shared their belief. They had a book to tell them what to believe in and a place to go check into each week to keep them on track. They were able to say that they were right, so right that they were *absolutely* right. They were able to think that there was no other way to be right. I had come to distrust religion (even though I knew people who were churchgoing but not intolerant and arrogant) and I despised the kind of zealotry shown by Jed and Megan. But I felt that I could not define myself purely by what I was not. I had to think about what I was. I had been thinking so hard about what I wasn't and about what I didn't want to be, I had not left time or energy to think about what I was or how I could describe what I did believe in.

I thought often about the Towers falling and all the people in them who knew they were going to die. I thought about the people on the top floors who called on their cell phones to say good-bye to their families. They were trapped, they all said, and they were waiting for help. They would be home soon, they hoped, and they all ended with "I love you" or "Kiss the kids for me." But they must have known that they weren't getting out. They must have realized soon after they made those calls that there was no hope of rescue or survival.

I played the scene over and over in my head. The room

is filling with thick, black smoke. The exits are all blocked, the down staircases are not passable, and the up staircases are locked so there is no way to get to the roof. I picture myself sitting, crouching really, near a window that has been broken open so we can breathe. The city stretches out before us, yet disappears through the thickening smoke. All around me are strangers. What are we doing? My friend Laura said she would be praying (she is Christian, so she means praying to God), but I am not, I could not be. I see myself getting to the bar and pouring myself a big martini, in one of the Windows on the World fancy glasses. And I see myself getting to the kitchen to find a big, luscious pastry, a beautiful piece of cake. I see myself sitting on the plush barstool, sipping vodka from a thin-rimmed glass and eating a marvelous sweet as I wait for the end of my world.

I want a cocktail party to usher me out. I want other people sitting next to me, perfect strangers perhaps, but other humans. And I want to clink glasses with them and toast to our existence, even as it is about to end. I want to look into the eyes of these other doomed souls as I fall with the Towers, as I am crushed by so much steel and concrete. I want to feel another hand in mine and die knowing that I am not alone.

Because I realize that people are all I really have. Other people are what make my life. They give it meaning. The interactions with other people bring me a wealth of emotions and confirm my place in the world. It is other people who make that place for me, each person shifts and turns to allow me in, to make space for me in this crowded world. These people are my family—they are nearest to me and mean the most to me. These people are my friends, my acquaintances, my neighbors—even the smallest nod of the head in greeting counts as interaction and adds to the experience of my day.

I could never value gods above humans. I could never prefer to spend time with deities and miss opportunities to connect with people. My sister-in-law once told me that God was more important to her than her own son. I spent months trying to figure out how that could be true. And I still puzzle over it. I cannot even think that there is a God who would want us to care more about him than our own offspring.

My children have challenged me lately. They have asked me, "Mommy, what do we believe in?" And I have answered with confidence that we believe in the human spirit, the strength and regenerative possibilities of people. And the kids ask, "What about God and Jesus?" So I say that I do not believe in God and I do not believe that Jesus was the son of God. I have gained the confidence to answer these questions through thinking, long, hard thinking. I had to figure out how to present the lack of religion in our lives as positive, as something we can be proud of. We may not have a church, but we have community, and we work hard to help our neighbors and strengthen our neighborhood. I want my children to feel good about who they are and what they believe in; I do not want them to fear the absence of religion, feel that they are wrong, or be ashamed of being nothing.

Amelia once told me with great certainty that God made the world, all the houses, the people, and even the sun. Another time she declared that she did not believe in God but that she did believe in Jesus. Both times I nodded with interest and allowed her to have her musings. Victor always wanted to know about churches and what they are for. However, when we did have the opportunity to attend an Easter service with his Californian grandparents, he hated it. He especially disliked the sermon and found one of the parables to be so ridiculous that he has made it into a family joke. He only needs to say, "There was a chicken and an eagle . . ." and we all giggle, even though we do acknowledge that the chicken was meant to be mankind and the eagle represented Christ, or maybe it was the other way around. Victor went through a phase during which he wanted to wear a tiny crucifix around his neck like some of the kids in his class, and he became upset when some of those kids told him he would go to hell for not going to church. He has learned to refuse to discuss his ideas with those kids and he has become certain that God does not exist. His certainty surprises me, mostly because when I was his age, I was so frightened and unsure. I am pleased with his statements like "God didn't make the world, and even if he did, he's dead, now!" or his most recent favorite, "Do you swear to Dog?"

My children have what I did not, they have a sense of security about what they are, what they believe in. They are not afraid of nothing, they accept it and see it as a way to keep open to the possibilities in the world. They see wonder and mystery in life, love, and even in death. They do not want the explanations given by religion and they do not see our way as frightening, isolating, or as a void waiting to be filled.

Through helping the children find respect for their beliefs, I have had to find respect for mine and tolerance for others, even for those who cannot tolerate me. I try to expose my family to all religions, even long-extant ideas have relevance to me. I have tried to explain to the kids why there are some who cannot tolerate us, why there are people who see us as enemies of our own country. I have become stronger in the face of such intolerance; I have become more secure about who I am. I have come to embrace the term *nothing*. I like it and use it to let people know, if they ask, that I am not a "believer." I prefer it to other terms because it is stark, it stands alone—without referring to gods or religion—and it is funny. Of course I am not really "nothing"; I believe in many things and have even decided that terms like *truth*, *faith*, and *grace* can have meaning to me in my own way. But when I say I am nothing, and when my kids say it, too, I feel proud and I breathe deeply with inner peace.

Of course, the inner peace is fleeting; the kids often ask for more information, clarification, or reiteration about this topic. So I smile at them when they ask again, "Mommy, what are we?" I feel full of faith and truth as I look at them and into their eyes, the eyes that I created and that reflect me so perfectly, and I say, "Let's find out together."